Some Aspects of Medieval Indian History

SOME ASPECTS
OF
MEDIEVAL INDIAN HISTORY

U. N. DAY

LOW PRICE PUBLICATIONS
Delhi-110052

Distributed by
D.K. Publishers Distributors (P) Ltd.
4834/24, Ansari Road, Darya Ganj,
New Delhi-110002
Phones: 23278584, 23278368, 232614
e-mail: dkpd@del3.vsnl.net.in
url: www.dkpd.com

First Published 1971
Second Edition 1990
Reprinted in **LPP** 1993, 1998, 2004

Upendra Nath Day (1913-)

ISBN 81-7536-341-X

Published by
Low Price Publications
A-6, Nimri Commercial Centre,
Near Ashok Vihar Phase-IV,
Delhi-110052
Phones: 27401672, 27452453
e-mail: lpp@nde.vsnl.net.in
url: www.lppindia.com

Printed at
D K Fine Art Press P Ltd.
Delhi-110052

PRINTED IN INDIA

Preface to the Second Edition

I have re-examined all the essays included in the first edition and could find no cause to alter my views as expressed in them. Except for some minor changes the text of the present edition is substantially the same as in the first edition. In spite of all cares some printing mistakes still might have crept in and for this I crave the indulgence of the readers.

S 19/53, Varuna Bridge
Varanasi-221002.

U.N. Day

Preface to the First Edition

Some Aspects of Medieval Indian History is a selection from my essays and articles based on my lectures to the post-graduate classes. Presistent demand to possess them in permanent form led me to collect them together in a book form. A few of these essays have already appeared in one or the other Research Journal, though in their present form they have been slightly altered and revised. Others are written exclusively for this study. These essays try to re-examine and re-interpret some of the controversial topics of Medieval Indian History. In these essays I have expressed my views without any reservations with a view to share them with the student of history. A glance through the pages will indicate that my views differ, often radically, from the commonly accepted ones, and I am sorry if I have inadvertently hurt the feelings of any one. But then in interpreting history one should be free from prejudices and ideologies, and I shall welcome and sincerely appreciate any helpful criticism.

I also take this opportunity to thankfully acknowledge the help I have received from Shri Om Prakash Sharma and Shri R.S. Mathur in preparing the press copy and the index.

Delhi:
15th August, 1971. U.N. Day

Contents

1

The Sultanate and the Caliphate

A problem which often puzzles a student of the Medieval Indian history is the position of the Sultanate of Delhi *vis-a-vis* the Caliphate. It has become a problem because the interpretations offered by scholars do not stand the test of evidence beyond a certain superficial point. Scholars agree on the view that the Sultanate was, theoretically, a part of the Caliphate and in support of this view they invariably refer to the often repeated legends that are found on coins issued by the sultans of Delhi. Prof. Arnold seems to have taken the lead in this line of thinking. At one place he mentions that "just as the Prophet is the vicegerent of God and the Caliph the vicegerent of the Prophet, the monarch is the vicegerent of the Caliph." At another place he says that "no king of the east or the west can hold the title of Sultan unless there be a covenant between him and the Caliph."[1] Prof. Qureshi holds the view that "in the eastern lands of Islam the legal position of the Abbasids were unquestioned, that no monarchy considered itself legally established without recognition by the Commander of the Faithful." "Thus no area where the Caliph was recognised could be legally independent. Even the rulers of states on whom he was practically dependent were legally subordinate to him. *Dejure* he was the sovereign, no one could rule without his consent."[2] Recently the same view has been reiterated by another scholar who mentions that on the basis of numismatic evidence one may assume that the authority of the Abbasid Caliph was accepted practically throughout the period of pre-Mughal rule in India. as the source and sanction of the Sultan's legal authority."[3]

The above conclusions aim at establishing a juridico-political unity under the Abbasid Caliphate and also that

---

1. Arnold, *Caliphate*, pp. 73, 74, 101, 102.
2. Qureshi, *Administration of the Sultanate of Delhi*, pp. 24, 25.
3. Aziz Ahmad, *Islamic Culture In Indian Environment* (Oxford, 1964), p. 11.

there was some thing like Pan-Islaism during the period prior to the establishment of the Mughal rule in India. The question to be examined, therefore, is that how far the Sultans of Delhi considered the authority of the Abbasid Caliphs as the source and sanction of their legal authority and also if they ever considered their kingdom as a part of the Empire of the Caliph. To understand the circumstances that led to the rise of the Turks within the fold of the Abbasid Caliphate it would be useful to make a rapid survey of the trends and the strands that worked in the dominions of the Abbasid Caliphate which gave rise to racial, cultural and religious conflict, a conflict which was brought to India as a legacy by the Turks.

The Abbasids had come to the pontifical position of the Caliph by espousing the cause of the Alids and by enlisting the support of the Persians, a section of the Arabs of the south and other non-Arab elements within the fold of the Islamic community. On the fall of the last Ommayyad, Abul Abbas the '*Saffiah*' (750-54) successfully manoeuvered to set aside the Alids and getting himself elected as the Caliph. Inspite of his cruelty and ferocity in wrecking vengience upon the Ummayyads, '*Saffah*' was regarded as a generous sovereign' attentive to his duties and not given to self indulgence.[4] Besides, his mild and tolerent attitude towards the Alids in Particular and the Shi'ites in general appeased them for the time being. His successor Abu Jafar Al Mansur (754-75), however, was a man of different temper. With a rare foresight he laid the foundations of an organisation which maintained and enhanced the prestige of the pontifical throne, and in later years became the chief source of strength and the main stay of its influence. "The permanence of the family, the power they weilded and the influence they exercised, even after they had lost their temporal sovereignty" were the results of his organisational ability. But he was "cold blooded, calculating and unscrupulous" and "spared none whom he thought in

---

4. Amir Ali, *A Shori History of the Saracens*, p. 209.

any way dangerous to himself or to his dynasty."[5] Before Mansur the Abbasids and the Alids were united. But by his treatment of the descendants of Ali, Mansur brought about a clevage and made the Alids hostile towards the Abbasids. Mansur's attitude towards the Alids was an outcome of his own fear. During the years when the Ummayyad Caliphate was fast crumling the descendants of the Prophet had started taking interest in the course of events. At Madina a meeting was held at which most of the members of Banu Hashim including Mansur were present. The entire assembly including Mansur took an oath of fealty to Muhammad, a great grandson of Hasan, recognising him thereby as the Caliph. But when finally Mansur became the Caliph he could not forget his earlier oath and the meeting and remembered that there was a consensus of opinion in favour of Muhammad. This memory deepened his suspicion and he attempted to seize the persons of Muhammad and his brother Ibrahim, which resulted in their open hostility. The whole of Hajaz and Yemen accepted Muhammad as the Caliph ; even Imam Abu Hanifa and Imam Malik pronounced in favour of the validity of Muhammad's claim. Mansur however, succeeded in suppressing the uprising, and followed his success by wrecking vengience upon Banu Hassan and Banu Hussain. Madina and Basra bore the burnt of his wrath. Imam Abu Hanifa and Imam Malik both had to pay the price for their support by undergoing humiliation and suffering.

Mansur's suspicion and his conflict with the Shi'ites consisting of the Alids, the Banu Hassan and the Banu Hussain was mainly responsible for the Abbasids' dependence and reliance in the beginning on the Persians and then on the Turks. With the predominance of the Persians the Arab elements gradually receded into the background. Those who lived in the towns continued to serve the Caliph though in subordinate positions, but the Arabs of the country-side returned to the solitude of the desert and reverting to their wild ways they began to take part in insurrections and

---

5. *ibid.*, pp. 212, 213.

revolts. The Persian domination was gradually replaced by Turks. From the time of Caliph Mamun (813-33) onwards Turkish troops began to surround the Caliph and by the time of Caliph Mutasim (833-42) they gained complete influence over the Caliphate. Mutasim being born of a Turkish mother feared and despised the Persians and relied more on the Turks and employed them in such large numbers that "Baghdad became too small for them".[6] The Turkish guards soon became so powerful that they began to make and unmake the Caliphs at their sweet will.

While the Turkish domination over the Caliphate created discontentment among the Arabs, the Fatimid-Ismaili movement which was brewing in the territories of the Abbasid Caliphate offered them "a chance of canalising the whole social and religious discontent."[7] Ismailism as a movement grew out of scheism among the Shi'ites over the question of recognising the successor of Imam Jafar us Sadik. A Section of the Shi'ites refused to recognise Musa al-Kazim as Imam after the death of Imam Jafar and adhered to their earalier allegiance to Ismail the elder brother of Musa. This gave rise to Ismailism which finally culminated in founding the Fatimid Ismaili Caliphate in Cairo in 909 A.D.

The establishment of the Fatimid Caliphate at Cairo was a challenge to the Abbasid Caliphate. While the Abbasid Caliphate from the second half of the 9th Century became exclusively dominated by the Turks, the Fatimid Caliphate remained under the domination of the Arabs. Thus the "conflict of the two great medieval Muslim Caliphates—that of the Abbasids ruling from Baghdad and the Fatimids ruling from Cairo tended to become an Arab-Turkoman conflict within the complex of racial, religious and cultural influences."[8]

6. M. Habib, *Introduction to Elliot & Dowson*, II, p. 91.
7. Bernard Lewis, *Origins of Ismailism*, p. 2.
8. Abbas Hamdani, '*The Fatimid Abbasid conflict in India* Paper read at XXVI International Congress of Orientalist, New Delhi-1964

Abbasid Caliphate supplied the Turks with the necessary training and soon the genious of the race unfolded itself as conquerors, administrators and generals. Champions of Sunni Orthodoxy, the Turks became the mainstay of the Caliphate and boasted about it as a matter of pride. The position of the Turkish guards is well reflected in the following story. "The Caliph Mu'tazz (866-69) once summoned the astrologers and asked them how long he would live and retain the caliphate. A wit who was present said" I know better than the astrologers." Being asked to specify the period of the Caliph's rule he replied". "So long the Turks pleased."[9] According to Zurji Zaydan whereas at first the Turkish captains swore allegiance to the Caliph, presently the Caliph swore allegiance to them."[10]

That the association of the Turks with the Abbasid Caliphate became a matter of glorious tradition, a thing for the Turks to remember and boast about is reflected in *Rahat us Sudur* (completed in 1202-3) wherein the author boastfully exclaims that "in Arabia, Persia, Rum and Russia the sword is in the hands of the Turks, that religion learing and piety are flourishing under their protection, that irreligion, heresies schism etc. have been stamped out so that all paths are closed save the path of Muhammad." According to the author all this was in confirmity with the prophecy made earlier when in response to Imam Abu Hanifa's paryer to God that his doctrines might endure the answer came from the unseen world, "Thy doctrines shall not wane so long as the sword continues in the hands of the Turks."[11] Thus we fined that when the Turks began to found their independent kingdoms they associated the name of the Caliph more as a memory of their great past when the Caliph depended on their support than as a mark of their recognition of the Caliph as their suzerain and source of power. Mahmud of Ghazni was the

9. M. Habib, *Loc. cit.*, p. 32.
10. Quated by Habib *Loc. cit.*, p. 92.
11. Quated by Bhargava, '*A Sarvey of Islamic Culture and Institutions*, p. 73.

first Turkish ruler to receive a robe of honour from the Caliph. Utbi writes that 'Qadir Bi-llah Amir-ul-muminin, the Khalifa of Baghdad sent a *Khilat* such as had never been heard of, for the use of Sultan Saifud-daula and he entitled Mahmud in his imperial rescript, Yamin-ud daula Amin ul Milat, the friend of the Amir-ul-muminin which had not yet been bestowed upon any prince."[12] But to what extent Mahmud accepted Caliph Qadir Billah as his suzerain can be judged from the following incident. On Mamud's demand for Samarkand the Caliph replid "I will do no such thing and if you take prossession of Samarkand without my permission I will disgarce you before the whole world." Mahmud on receiving the reply became furious. "Do you wish me to come to the capital of the Caliphate with a thousand elephants," he said to the Caliph's envoy, "in order to lay it waste and bring its earth on the back of my elephants to Ghazni." Finally Mahmud did establish his power over Samarkand[13] and the Caliph had to remain a passive spectator. The above mentioned incident clearly indicates that Mahmud did not accept Caliph Qadir Billah as his suzerain nor did he require the Caliph's sanction for exercising his authority as Sultan. At best the Caliph was recognised as a symbol of Sunni orthodoxy.

The question, how far the Sultans of Delhi considered the authority of the Abbasid Caliphs as the source and sanction of their legal authority and also if they ever considered their kingdom as a part of the Caliphate may now be examined in the light of the above resume.

Among the Sultans of Delhi it was Iltutmish who first received a robe of honour from the Caliph of Baghdad, and according to Dr Tripathi "it not only fastened the fiction of Khilafat to the Sultanate to Delhi, but legally involved the recognition of final sovereignty of the Caliph."[14] Iltutmish

12. *Elliot*, II p. 24.
13. M. Habib, *Sultan Mahmud of Ghaznin*, p. 36.
14. Tripathi, *Some Aspects of Muslim Admlnistration* (1936), p. 26.

adopted the title of *Nasir Amir-ul-muminin*[15] which of course literally means that he claimed for himself only the position of a helper of the *Amir-ul-muminin* i.e. the Abbasid Caliph. But it dose not necessarily imply that he adopted such titles to proclaim to the Islamic world his recognition of the Caliph as his suzerian or his kingdom a part of the Caliphate. He did not hesitate to attack and subjugate Ghiysuddin of Bengal who had also received a similar robe of honour from the Caliph. His action indicates that the adoption of the *Nasir Amir-ul-muminin* was only a formal way of keeping a tradition which the Turks had adopted from Mahmud of Ghazni but absolutely free of any legal binding. It was a memory of the glorious past when the Turks were truely the helpers of the Caliph and on whose help the Caliphate depended for its existence hence a matter of pride and honour before the Muslim world.

The conduct of the subsequent sultans also indicate that the association of their names with the Caliphate was more an act of perpetuating a memory than a formal recognition of an authority beyond the bounds of their kingdom. The Caliphate of Baghdad was destroyed by Hulagu (1258) and even the person of the Caliph was not spared. Yet we find that when the emissaries of Hulagu visited India within two years of the sack of Baghdad a very hearty welcome was extended to them.[16] If the Caliph was recognised as the suzerain, certainly his destroyer should have been regarded as an enemy by the Sultan of Delhi, and the destroyer of the unity of the Caliphate, an underserving personality unworthy of friendship. That the Sultan could place political need above sentiment was made possible because there was no such sentiment or attachment as have been read in recent times.

---

15. Wright, H. N., *The Sultans of Delhi, Their Coinagc and Metrology*, p. 16 ; Thomas, Eddward, *The Chronicles of the Pathan Kings of Delhi*, p. 52.
16. *Tabaqa-it-Nasiri*, (*Elliot* II pp. 382-3).

Turning to the legends inscribed on the coins of the Mamluk Sultans we find that *Nasir Amir-ul-muminin* and Al Mustansir... *Amir-ul-muminin* which appeared on the coins of Iltusmish continued during the reigns of his successors. The name of Caliph Mustansir appeared on the coins of Rukn-ud-din-Firuz Shah (1236 A.D.), Jalalat-ud-din Raziyya (1236-1240 A.D.) Muiz-ud-din Bahram Shah (1240-1242 A.D.) and Alaud-din Masud Shah (1242-1246 A.D.). In the coins of Alaud-din Masud Shah the name of Al Musta'-sim appeared for the first time[17] and continued to appear subsequently in the coins of Nasir-ud-din Mahmud (1246-1266 A.D.), Ghiyas-ud-din Balban (1266-1287 A.D.) and Muizz-ud-din Kaiqbad (1287-1290 A.D.) though Musta'-sim's caliphate had come to an end in 1258 A.D.).

Coming to the Khaljis we find that the legends on the coins of Jalal-ud-din Khalji (1290-1296 A.D.) do not reflect any change from the previous tradition. The name of Caliph Al Musta'sim appears in the same traditional form—*Al Imam Al Musta'sim Amirul muminin,*[18] though he was already long dead. For himself Jalalud-din used the traditional form of Delhi Sultans such as Al Sultan ul Azam Jalal-ud-duniya wa-al-din Abul Muzaffar Firuz Shah Al Sultan. In his reign we have the interesting case of Sayyidi Maula who organised a conspiracy against the Sultan. While he thought of the throne of Delhi his followers thought of proclainming him as the Caliph.[19] If the Abbasid Caliph was recognised as the source and sanaction of authority for the Sultan of Delhi, the supporters of Sayyidi Maula certainly would not have thought of proclaiming him as the Caliph. It is a positive indication that to the common Indian Muslim Abbasid Caliphate had no meaning in politics. Barani who is credited with writing a treatise on Medieval Indian political Thought certainly would have been critical of such an attempt if the Caliph was recognised as the source and sanc-

---

17. Wright, *Loc. cit.*, p. 47 No. 189.
18. Thomas, *Loe. cit.*, No. 121.
19. Barani, *Tarikh-i-Firuz Shahi* (Bib. Ind. Text), p. 210.

tion of the Sultan of Delhi or in other words if the Caliph was recognised as the legal sovereign of India. Instead of of criticising Sayyidi Maula, Barani denounces Jalal-ud-din for executing the Maula.[20]

The legends found on the coins of Ala-ud-din Khalji are[21] : *Sikandar-us-Sani, Yamin-ul-Khilafat, Nasir Amirul-ul-muminin*. By the time of Alaud-din such titles had become almost a traditional matter of boasting rather than one having any real significance. At best they were attempts at perpetuating the memories of the glorious past of the Turks. It amounted to proclaiming that the Sultan belonged to that class which had been the chief prop of the Caliphate. Though Alaud-din did not claim for himsef the title of the Caliph his court poet Amir Khusrau unhesitatingly mentions him as the Caliph of the age.[22] Amir Khusrau who was quite conversant with the Islamic traditions would not have addressed Alaud-din Khalji as Caliph of the age if India was considered as a part of the Caliphate and the Abbasid Caliph as the source and sanction of Sultan's authority. We also find Alaud-din keen on keeping his diplomatic relations with the Il Khans of Persia who were associated with the destruction of Abbasid Caliphate and executioner of the person of the Abbasid Caliph. It at least indicates that the Sultan paid greater heed to the necessities of the politics than to mere sentiments.

Qutb-ud-din Mubarak Shah Khalji started with the customary legends which are found in his coins dated A.H. 716 where in the titles are as : *Sikandar-uz-zaman, Yamin-ul-khilafat, Nasir Amirul-muminin*. Subsequently, however he proclaimed himself as the Caliph and adoptad very high sounding titles. The titles found in his coins are : *Khilafat Ullah, Amir-ul-muminin, Imam-ul-'Azam, Khlifai Rbbul 'Alimiun*.[23] If

20. *ibid.*, p. 212.
21. Wright, *Loc. cit.*, p. 88 No.305; Thomas, *Loc. cit.*, p. 168
22. Amir Khusrau, *Khazain-ul Futuh* (Rizwi, p. 165).
23. Thomas, *Loc. cit.*,pp. 179-181, Wright, *Loc. cit.*, p. 97.

these titles had any positive implications Mubarak Shah certainly had none of the qualities to justify them. As if not content with these titles he adopted the pseudo-Abbasid ruling name alwasiq.[24] Mubarak Shah was not satisfied merely by appropriating these titles, but styled his capital Delhi as Darul Khilafat.

These pretentions of Mubarak Shah should have been censured by the Ulama of the age, if the Caliph was looked upon by the Indian Muslims as the source and sanction of authority of the Sultan of Delhi. Amir Khusrau proudly mentions of Delhi as Darul Khilafat, and Firuz Shah Tughlaq in his *Fatuhat* unhesitatingly mentions that he repaired the tomb of Mubarak Shah Khalji.[25] Muhammad Tughlaq made pilgrimages to his tomb and kissed his slippers, and appointed Ibn Battutta as the manager (*mutwalli*) of the endowments granted for the proper upkeep of the tomb.[26]

It is difficult to assess the motives of Sultan Mubarak Shah Khalji for his pretentions to Caliphate. Of course one may very well assign it to the caprice of the monarch, but as pointed out earlier, in that case it would have brought censure, at least after his death. While his private life and handling of the affairs of the state have received condemnation, his act of proclaiming himself as the Caliph and the leader of the Sunni community has received approbation. The suggestion that it was like a proclaimation of the liberation of Delhi Sultanate is also not tenable because, as pointed out earlier, Delhi was already free and since the destruction of Baghdad by Hulagu, the Abbasid Caliphate had become extinct.

The answer to his conduct may, however, be found in the political condition prevailing outside India. Last quarter of the thirteenth century witnessed the bad days of the Turks. The Byzantine and Mongol power had eclipsed them

24. Thomas, *Loc. cit.*, pp. 179, 192.
25. *Fatuhat-i-Firuzshahi*, p. 17.
26. Ibn Battutta, *Rehla*,

for the time being. But the Turks under the inspiring leadership of Osman after whom they are known as the Osmanli or the Ottoman Turks had recovered wonderfully in the opening decade of the fourteenth century. The conversion of Ghaaan Khan (1295-1304) no doubt was a great gain to Islam, but at the same time it introduced a new racial element into its fold. When Aljaitu Khudabanda (1304-16) the brother and successor of Ghazan Khan, adopted Shia faith,[27] it added religious tension to the racial hostility. With the Fatimid Ismaili pockets already exhisting in Sind under the independent dynasty of the Sumras who had been defying the Turks, the possibility of Shi'ite combination of the Mongols, Arabs and Sumras might have necessitated a vindication of their position by accepting Mubarak Shah as the Caliph—an institution which had been destroyed by the Ilkhanids.

Before we proceed to examine the rule of the Tughlaqs we may recount the activity of the Shi'ites in India which seem to have influenced the politics and the policies of the Tughlaqs. Shi'ism entered India during the Caliphate of Mu'atamid (872-892) when in his attempt to pacify a sections of the Persians he acquiesced to the occupation of Sind in 871 by the Safarid leader Yaqub bin Lays who spread Shi'ism in Sind. After the death of Yaqub in 878 Sind was devided into two independent territories of that of Multan and Mansura (Brahnanabad). During the period when the Arabs were striving hard to establish the Fatimid Caliphate in Egypt under the Ismaili inspiration, India was not neglected by them. In 883 they sent a mission under the Fatimid Da'e alHaysam[28] to establish contact with Multan and Mansura. Thence onwards it became regular practice of of sending Da'is to India. The process was more intensified from the time of the Fatimid Caliph alMu'izz (953-975) as a result of which their influence became marked in Multan. In

27. Sykes, *History of Persia,* II, p. 111 ; Carl Brokelmann, *History of the Islamic People*, p. 251.
28. *J.R.A.S.* 1930, pp. 516, 518, 522 ; *Tarikhi-Jahankushai.*

965 the Fatimid Dai's Jalan bin Shayban founded his own dynasty to rule in Multan. This Arab Ismaili state of Multan continued to exist till it was destroyed by the orthodox Sunni Turkish power of Ghazna under Mahmud in 1010-11. Till then it served as a buffer between the Rajput power of the Pratiharas and the Turkish power of Ghazna. The subjugation of Multan by Mahmud of Ghazna marks the beginning of the replacement of Arab Muslim rule in India by the Turkoman Muslim rule.[29] The other Ismaili State that of Mansura where the Arab dynasty of Habbari Quarayshids had been ruling was also swept aside by Mahmud while returning from his Somnath compaign in 1056.

With the breakdown of the political power of Multan and Manśura, the Ismaili activity did not come to an end They found a strong foot-hold at Thatta where the Sumras had succeeded in establishing their independent kingdom in 1051 A.D. during the reign of Ghaznhvide Abdur Rashid.[30] The Sumras were local Hindu tribes but had accepted Islam and had intermarried with the Arabs. They had come under Ismaili influence sometimes about 1034 and had remained Ismaili since then. Under the Ismaili influence they began to consider themselves as Alids.[31]

With the rise of the Samsbaniya dynasty of Ghur, the Turks focused their attention towards Delhi and the Doab ; Sind was practically forgotten. This gave ample opportunity to the Ismailis to consolidate their hold over the people through the rule of the Sumras. Thus while northern India passed through the conquest of the Turks the Sumras maintained their Ismaili Shi'ism for about three centuries and were still in Thatta when Muhammad bin Tughlaq invaded that region in 1351.

This brief resume will show that while the Turks were championing the cause of orthodox Sunni creed, the

29. Abbas Hamdani *Loc. Cit.*
30. *Tarikh-i-Masumi,* (Poona-1938) p. 60.
31. Abbas Hamdani, *Beginning of Ismailism in Northern India*, p. 9.

Shi'ites were not absolutely idle, their Ismaili sect was dominating the region of Sind. Thus the Fatimid-Abbasid conflict had turned into Arab-Turkoman conflict in India.[32] The Arabs had also a number of settlements in different port towns and were carrying on over sea trade in their own vessels. The existence and activities of Shi'ite Arabs, and the Arab oriented Ismaili sects in India seems to have been an important factor that led the Turkish Sultans of Delhi to proclaim time and again their association with the Abbasid Caliphate representing the orthodox Sunni community and the glorious days of the Turks.

Ghiyasuddin Tughlaq, who had taken up the cause of the orthodox Sunni[33] against the rule of Nasiruddin Khusrau Shah, could not think of proclaiming himself as the Caliph on his accession to the throne. He was conscious of the opposition that he had to face even for becoming a Sultan, and certainly was conscious that a claim of being a caliph would be too much. On his coins, therefore, he claimed to be only *Nasir-Amir-ul-muminin*. We have already noticed that the title of *Amir-ul-muminin* and the Caliph had been adopted by Mubarak Shah Khalji to whom Tughlaq Shah proclaimen his loyalty, and there is no reason to believe that Tughlaq Shah aimed at a non-existing Caliph, and not as helper to his master who had also been recognised as the Caliph. Dr. Tripathi, has rightly concluded that "so much fuss for an unworthy prince obviously lacks sincerity, and seems to have been intended not for his soul but for the

---

32. The idea has been fully developed and discussed by Prof. Abbas Hamdani in his paper *"The Fatimid Abbasid conflict in India."*
33. Barani, *Loc Cit.*, p. 415. Barani speaks of Sufi Khan, one of the supporters of Nasiruddin Khusrau Shah as a Mulahid and also mentions tbat on Sufi Khan's requesting the fakirs for his victory against Ghazi Malik, these fakirs prayed to God to grant victory in the battle between the Barwars and Ghazi Malik to the side that championed the cause of the true religion of Muhammad.

advertisemedt of the Tughlaqs."[34] Who knows the adoption of the title *Nasir Amir-ul-muminin* too was not another form of this advertisement.

Muhammad Tughlaq started his reign with a different note. Being a rationalist he could understand the superficiality of reference to the Caliphate which had become meaningless. It is also not very unlikely that being desirous of establishing diplomatic relations with the Memeluk Sultan al Nasir of Egypt, Ilkhanid Abu said of Persia, and Chagatai Tarmashirin of Transoxiana he contidered it expedient not to refer to the Caliphate which had different connotations in those regions. Thus in the coins that he issued in his own name, the *Kalima* (the Muslim confession of faith) the date and mint name appear on the obverse, and on the reverse his own name with Caption *'Al Mujahid fi Sabilullah'* and the names of first four Caliphs are found.[35] On his coins of smaller denominations he instituted such captions as 'Sovereignty is not conferred upon every man but is placed on the elect' ; He who obeys the Sultan truely obeys God ; "The Sultan is the shadow of the God ; "God is the supporter of the Sultan etc."[36]

Though rebellion and uprising was a common feature of the Turkish rule, from 1335 onwards upto his death Muhammad Tughlaq was confronted with a series of rebellions which were far wide spread and interconnected with each other. The ring leaders of these rebellions belonged to two groups. The first group consisted of the officers of the state and the second group consisted of a class of people who had hitherto enjoyed sanctity consisting of the *Ulama*, the *Qazis*, the *Khatibs* (Preachers) and *Faqihs* (Jurists) and the *Masaikh*.[37]

34. Tripathi, *Loc cit.*, p. 59.
35. Thomas, *Loc. cit.*, p. 208.
36. The view that Muhammad Tughlag wanted to educate the people through the captions on his coinage is questionable because the language of such captions is a difficult one which the common people certainly could not have understood.
37. Mehdi Husain, *The Tughlaq Dynasty*, p. 261.

At the root of the these rebellions lay the attempt of Muhammad Tughlaq at over-centralisation of the administration—a measure which led to curtailment of the powers of the nobles, and hence their resentment. But when Muhammad Tughlaq tried to control the Ulama and the Mashaikh first by offering them and then compelling them to take up government services, he offended the class which wielded great influence over the Muslim masses. Thus by his stern and tactless behaviour he indirectly brought about a combination of these different interest groups. It became almost a vicious circle. The more stern and ruthless the Sultan became the more resolute and wide spread became the resistence.

Such a combined and almost simultaneous uprising, the impact of which was felt all over the kingdom, could not have been brought about without some preaching and 'propa ganda' on the part of the Ulama, the Khatibs. and the Mashaikh. The Qazis gave verdict against Muhammad Tughlaq that he had revolted against Islam and had joined hands with the 'non-believers' (*Jumrah-i-Kufar*) and had thus forfeited his life.[38]. Barani casts doubt about Muahmmad Tughlaq's belief which also indicates the line of attack against him by the Ulama and the Mashaikh. Writing about the influences on Sultan Muhammad's thought Barani says that he spent his younger days in the company of such irreligious persons and philosophers as Sad-ud-din Mantaki, poet Ubaid and Najm-ud-din Inteshar, and that later he used to spent hours in the company of philosopher[39] Alimud-din. Ibn Battutta also mentions Muhammad Tughlaq's discourses in philosophy ; "I have seen at the court of the Indian Emperor Sultan Muha mmad philosophical matters alone being discussed every day after morning prayer."[40] According to

---

38. Isami *Futuh-us-Salatin*, verses 9748-53 ; Rizwi, *Tughlaq Kalin Bharat*, I, p. 118.
39. Barani, *Loc. cit.*, p. 465.
40. Ibn Battuta, *The Rehla*, p. 266.

Barani, these persons who were followers of *Maqulat* (reason) and always talked of reason, influenced the mind of the Sultan so much that he developed disbelief for the Sunni religion' the prophets and the revealed books. He lost his faith in the book of the Prophet (Quran) and the Hadis. If his mind had not been influenced by these persons he would never have acted against Islam.[41] In the beginning Muhammad Tughlaq was not perturbed by these rebellions. His attitude is well reflected in the following statement of Barani that the Sultan said, "I am not at all perturbed by these rebellions. I am aware of the gossip that the rebellions are due to the exceeding bloodshed, caused by the Sultan. But I am not prepared to give up *Siyasat* on account of such gossip nor on account of the out-break of rebellions."[42] The Ulama and the Qazis had no difficulty in proclaiming the repressive measures of Muhammad Tughlaq as anti-Islamic because "the Shari'at took no cognizance of crimes against state"[43]

The verdict of the Ulama that Muhammad Tughlaq had devited from the right path (Sunni creed) if read along with the existence of a number of Ismaili pockets and their activities in Western India, will indicate that the Ulama might have pronounced a verdict on the Sultan's stress on reason as an outcome of Mutazilite influence and an indication of his leaning towards shi'ism.

Muhammad Tughlaq, having discovered that his repressive measures were not successful in curbing the disturbances behind which there was wide spread propaganda about his faith, thought of a counter move. He struck upon the idea that a certificate from the Abbasid Caliph who was regarded as the symbol of Sunni creed would convince his subjects that he was an upholder of the Sunni creed and thereby counteract the propaganda of the Ulama, the Qazis and the Khatibs. The Statements of Barani, Ibn Battutta, and even the so-called

41. Barani, *Loc. cit.*, pp. 465.
42. *ibid.*. p 509.
43. Mahdi Husain, *Loc. cit.*, p. 344.

autobiography of Muhammad bin Tughlaq become intelligible when read in this context.

In his characteristic way, once Muhammad Tughlaq conceived the idea he atonce started working upon it He started with the propaganda about his search for the Abbasid Caliph, which was aimed at circulating the news about the Sultan's belief. It is highly improbable that he had no information about the resuscitated Abbasid Caliphate in Cairo particularly when he was already having communication with al Nasir the Mamaluk Sultan of Egypt. The suspension of the 'Id and Friday prayers were aimed at the same direction. The discontinuation of the prayers followed by their resumption would atonce attract the attention of the people towards any change that might be introduced. The next step of issuing coins[44] in the name of the Abbasid Caliph al Mustakfi and the reading of the khutba in the name of the Caliph were introduced by the Sultan to proclaim his adherence to the Sunni creed and a counter-move to the propaganda of the Ulama. He must have reasoned out that a declaration of his faith from his side would not have the same weight as one declared by the Caliph through his recognition. With this end in view he had been communicating with the Caliph for about two or three months when he was at Sargdwari and when Haji Sarsari came to Delhi, from Egypt, bringing to the Sultan, the letter mandate (*mansur*) the Caliphal insignia (*Liva*) and the robe (*Khilat*) from the Caliph,[45] he crossed almost all limits to display humility to the Caliph.

---

44. Muhammad Tughlaq's coins can be classified into five categories: (i) Those issued in memory of his father recording only the latter's name (ii) Those struck in his own name—the normal series (iii) Those issued as forced currency (iv) Those recording the names of Abbasid Caliph al Mustakfi I and al Hakim II, the caliph issue (v) Those issued as suzerain of Bengal. Wright, Loc. cit., pp. 122 ff.
45. Barani, *Loc. cit.*, p. 492.

That all this display of loyalty to the Caliph was only a political stunt and a counter-move to thwart the propaganda of the Ulama did not remain hidden to those who were also using religion as a means for furthering their. cause The expression of Barani and Ibn Battutta that every body was surprised to witness the acts of humility of the Sultan towards the Caliph, in fact refers to the understanding smile of those who were most concerned with it.

These changes neither compromised the political independence of the Sultan in any way, nor do they indicate that Muhammad Tughlaq was "the first pan-Islamist in India who believed in the world of Islam as a composit totality, at the centre of which was the authority of the Abbasid Caliph, [46] as Aziz Ahmad would have us believe. Nor even do they indicate that there was any idea of pan-Islamism then prevelant in India. On the contrary, these steps of Muhammad Tughlaq and the subsequent reaction of those who were opposed to him indicate the hollowness of the claims of the world of Islam as a composit totality with the authority of the Abbasid Caliph as its centre. Muhammad Tughlaq wanted to use the name of the Caliph as counter move against the propaganda of the Ulama and as a proof of his faith in Sunni creed, which however failed to achieve its end. The name of the Caliph as 'Talisman' proved inefficacious in preventing rebellions and clearly lays bare that Muslims in India had long ceased to think of the Abbasid Caliph as of any consequence in their political activities.

So far Muhammad Tughlaq is concerned he too realised the ineffectiveness of the Cairene Caliphate and regretted his hasty step. For, when he secured as a visitor a scion of the line of Abbas in the person of Ghiyas-un-din Muhammad, a great grandson of Khalifa Al Mustansir Billah, he realised that he could have proclaimed Gyiyas-ud-din Muhammad as Caliph[47] and thus resuscitated the Abbasid Caliphate with

46. Aziz Ahmad, *Loc. Cit.*, p. 8.
47. Ibn Battutta, (Rizwi, T. K. B. I, p. 197).

seat in Delhi and thereby proclaiming himself to the Muslim world as a champion of the Sunni creed and also having the puppet Caliph directly under his own control to be placed in the forefront against the Ulama. But in this sphere too like others, his action lost its vigour after meeting defeat and he devoted himself with greater sternness to suppress the rebellious spirit by force.

Muhammad Tughlaq, however, left as a legacy the Caliphal name, which Firuz Tughlaq with the weakness in his succession could ill-afford to discontinue. His title to the throne was based on election, but the election was only partial in which only a section, of course backed by the anti-Muhammad Tughlaq element, had voted for him[48]. Firuz Tughlaq's entire reign is an attempt at a compromise with the Ulama and the Mashaikh, and he might have considered the discontinuation of the reference to the Khalifa may offened the feelings of the orthodox group, whereas the continuation may possibly be advantageous to him particularly when he knew that the Caliph except as a symbol of sunni orthodoxy had no authority in India. The statement of Firuz Shah that "no king is secure until he has submitted himself to the khalifa" is typical of the religious twist that Firuz Shah gave in justification of his political activities.

There seems to have been a sudden accelaration in the shi'ite activities in northern India during the reign of Firuz Tughlaq. The character of these activities and the measures taken by Firuz can be found in his *Futuhat*[49] wherein he mentions that :—

---

48. Barani, *Loc.*, pp. 535-6. Barani has fabricated the story of Firuz Shah's nomination as a successor, just to point him as a legal successor of Muhammad Tughlaq and not an usurpur. We must remember that Barani was trying to win the favour of Firzu Shah through his *Tarikh*.

49. *Futuhat-i-Firuzshahi*, pp 6, 7.

(i) The seat of the Shi'as all called *Rawafiz*[50] had endeavoured to make proselytes. They wrote treatises and books and gave instructions and lectures upon tenets of their sect and reviled the pious Khalifas, (*Khitafat-i-Rashidin*) Ummul-muminin Hazrat Aisha and all prominent and great sufis."

"I (Firuz) seized them all and on the most jealous I inflicted punishment and the rest I visited with censure and threats of public punishment. Their books I burnt in public and so by grace of God the influence of this sect was entirely suppressed."

(ii) "There was a sect of heretics (mulahids and abahtiyas) who laboured to seduce people into heresy and schism (*Ithad* and *Itahat*). I executed their leaders who were shi'as and imprisoned and banished the rest, and thus their mischief was totally purged out of the Islamic kingdom".

(iii) "There was a sect which in the garment of atheism, renunciation and celebacy (Tajrid) used to mislead people. The head of this group was Ahmad Behari, who lived in the city of Delhi. In the region of Behar some called him God. One of his disciples affirmed that a God has appeared in Delhi, that is Ahmad Behari. When these facts were proved against them, I ordered them to be confined and punished with chains.[51] I admonished the others to repent and reform and banished them to different cities to put a stop to the influences of this wretched sect."

(iv) Besides these, one called Ruknuddin declared himself Mahdi and proclaimed that "I am that Mahdi after the appearance of whom the world will come to an end (Mahdi

---

50. The word Rawafiz is used for the followers of the sect of Ali, denominated Shi'ites
51. Sufi Saint Sharfuddin Yahiya Manairi's reaction to the news of Ahmad Behari's execution was not of joy but of sorrow. 'I shall be astonished if the city where the blood of such persons is spilt, endures prosperity for long. "Rizwi,—*T. K. B.* II, p. 331.

Akhirul-Zaman)." He led people astray into mystic practices and perverted ideas by maintaining that he was Rukn-ud-din, the prophet of God. The elders brought the facts of this case to my attention, and gave evidence of what they heard him say. When he was brought before me I investigated the charges of error and pervesion brought against him and he was convicted of heresy and error. The doctors of law (Ulama-i Din) gave the verdict that he was an infidel and worthy of death for having speard such vile and pervicious idea among the people of Islam. It was pointed out that if any delay were made in puttidg down such ideas they would spread like pestilence and many Musalmans would stray away from the true faith. A revolt would follow and many men would fall into perdition. I ordered that this vile fellow's rebellion and wickedness should be communicated to all societies of learned men (Ulama-i-Din) and be made public to all men high and low, and that in accordance with the decision of the Ulama the guilty should be brought to punishment...Upon hearing or reading of facts here recorded, every well wisher of the Prophet's religion will admit that this sect was deservedly punished, and for this good action I hope to receive future reward"[52]

"Another person who was the son of a liberated slave of Ain-ul-Mahru, set himself up as a Shaikh in Gujrat and having got together a body of disciples used to say *Anal Haq*. He claimed "I am that great force which never dies." He composed a treatise containing his words of Kufr...I condemned him to punishment, and his book I orderd to be burnt, so that his innovation might be prevented from spreading among the faithful people of Islam."

The above account as given by Firuz Shah indicates that the Shi'ite activity in his reign had become dangerous to the

52. The extent of the influence of these sects can be judged from the tone of the statement of Firuz Shah wherein he makes an attempt to convince the need of his strong or drastic measures to crush the activities of these sects.

State. The sudden explosion of Shi'ism possibly could have been due to two factors. First, the rationalistic approach of Muhammad Tughlaq and the stress given by him on reasoning might have encouraged some thinkers to question some aspects of the religion as propounded by the Ulama. The question of succession of Ali and the part played by Ummul Muminin Aisha in the politics against Ali, or the question that the Quran as it was obtained was the compilation of Caliph Osman or casting doubt about the prophethood of Muhammad by Ahmad Behari, are only a few examples of the doubts or questions raised by these people, who were not prepared to follow the Ulama bindly. The second factor might have been the overthrow of the Ismaili Shi'ite Sumras by the Sunni Samas in Sind. The Shi'ite Sumras provided an abode and an assylum to the Shi'ites, but when they were crushed and their kingdom lost to the Sunni power, the Shi'as escaped to various places as refugees, and started organising themselves and proselytising for increasing the followers of their faith by holding meetings etc.

Firuz Tughlaq, who had seen the strength of religious propaganda against a monarch during the reign of Muhammad Tughlaq considered it expedient to disperse and crush these Shi'ite activities before they took shape and dimentions. In his *Futuhat,* Firuz says, "God in His mercy and favour, made me His humble creature, the instrument of putting down such wickedness and abolishing such heresy, and guided me to effect a restoration of true religion."[53] To counteract the effects of the propaganda of these persons Firuz Tughlaq thought it necessary to keep the Ulama and the Mashaikh satisfied by seeking their approval of his actions, and to proclaim to his subjects his belief in the orthodox Sunni creed which was to be deemed as the State religion, and continued to retain the name of the Abbasid Caliphs, who had by convention come to be regarded as the symbol of Sunni faith.

---

53. *Futuhat-i- Firuzshahi,* p. 8.

Firuz Tughlaq received twice the robe of honour from the Abbasid Calipn of Cairo. These robes come unsolicited and indicates the Caliph's desire to display to the Muslim world his prestige rather than Firuz Tughlaq's anxiety to get the support of the Caliph to buttress his position as a Sultan. While restoring the names of the previous sultans in the *Khutba* of the Friday and the Id prayers, Firuz Shah included the name of Qutb-ud-din Mubarak Shah Khalji.[54] The inclusion of the name of a sultan who had claimed for himself the position of the Caliph, the *Amir-ul-muminin*, certainly contradicts his declaration "that no king is secure until he has submitted himself to the Khalifa" (the Abbasid caliph). If the Caliph or the Caliphate had any authoritative bearing on the Sultanate of Delhi, Firuz Tughlaq as a pious and religious monarch surely would not have included the name of Mubarak Shah Khalji in the *Khutba*.

Barani, who as a historian considered it his duty to give explanation or cause of every phenomenon, failing to understand the reason for peace and prosperity of the regin of Firuz Tughlaq assigned it to the blessings of the Caliph.[55] The statement of Barani, to a greater measure is responsible for creating the impression of the authority of the Caliph, though in reality it hardly ever existed in India.

The coins of Firuz Tughlaq include the names of Caliphs, Al Hakim (1340-53), Al Mu'tajid (1353-61) Al Mutawakkil (1361-83) The Caliphate of Al Mu'tajid lasted upto 1361 yet in the gold coin of Firuz dated 1364 his name appears with the epithet "*Khaladat Khilafathu*" i.e. "May his Caliphate remain in perpetuity". Similarly the name of Caliph Abu Abudullah al Mutawakkil whose caliphate ended in 1383 continued to appear on the coins of Firuz Shah and his successors[56] with the epithet "*Khaladat Khilafathu*" though he

54. Afif, *Tarikh-i-Firuzshahi*, p. 107
55. Barani, *Loc. cit.*, pp. 598-9
56. Thomas, *Loc. cit.*, pp 274-7, 304-5, 308-9. 311, 316 ; Wright, *Loc. cit.*, 172, 174, 210

was already dead for some time. Thus the appearance of the name of the Caliph cannot be taken as a conclusive proof of recognition of Caliphal authority either by Firuz Shah or his successors. The continuty of the name and the epithet had become matters of convention and were used as traditional numismatic decorations.

The legends on the coins of the Sayyid sultans hardly convey any particular meaning except that they were being simply used for decorative purpose without having any significance. They often used the available obverse dies of their predecessors[57] and hence the legends get all mixed up. The practice of using old available dies continued in the times of the Lodis and therefore nothing definite can be deducted from the legends. One thing however is worth noting that there is no evidence to show any kind of relationship with the Abbasid Caliphate of Cairo.

Sher Shah departed from the tradition that had come in vogue after Muhammad Tughlaq, and seem to have taken inspiration from the legends that were found on the coins of Muhammad Tughlaq (Personal series). He introduced the Qalima and the names of the first four Caliphs (Pious Caliphate) in his coins which became the Sur style and was continued by his successors Islam Shah, Muhammad Adil Shah and other pretenders.[58]

---

57. Thomas, *Loc. cit.*, p. 329

58. Wright, *Loc. cit.* p. 269.
The Sayyids and the Afghans (Lodis and Surs) did not profess association with the Abbasid Caliphate as will be seen from their coins. Similarly among the provincial kingdoms, the Sultans of Gujarat, the Bahmani rulars (and later the five kingdoms) also do not make any such proclaimation. It is only in the Sultans of Malwa who were Turks that we find recurrence of the similar profession.

Form the above narrative following points emerge :

1. That amongst the Sultans of Delhi only the Turks associated the names of the Caliph or referred to the Abbasid Caliphate in their coins.

2. That on the western borders of India the exhistence of Shi'ite Fatimid Ismaili pockets had tended to become Turko-Arab Conflict. The Turks representing the Sunni creed and the Arbas representing the Shi'ite creed.

3. That the Abbasid Caliphate was recognised as a symbol sunni faith.

4. That often the old dies (mostly obverse) were used with slight modification in the dates, and thus some legends on the coins continued to appear for considerable periods.

Thus to conclude we can say that in India, it is only the Sunni Turkish sultans who from time to time associated the Abbasid caliphate with their names, that such an association was not to proclaim their acceptance of the Abbasids as the source and sanction of their authority, nor that by this association the Sultans ere maintaining the idea of unity of Islam. They associated the Abbasid Caliphate with their names only to commemorate the glorious past of the Turks when the Caliphate depended on their support.

2

The North-West Frontier of the Sultanate

A. Under the Ilbari Turks*

The physical features of India are such that the problem of defence is much minimised, and, it was more so during the ages when scientific invention had not provided mankind with so many instruments of destruction. Of the frontiers of India, the one of the north-west had played the most significant role in the history of the sub-continent. It is through the passes situated in this region that the various races came to India, fought against the inhabitants, overpowered them and got mixed up into the multitude of people called the Indians. Nature, however, has provided this region of the north-west with a chain of continuous mountains, which offer the phenomenon of a natural frontier. This natural frontier is formed by the region consisting of the Kirthar range, the Sulaiman mountains, the slopes of Hindukush and the Himalayas. In short, it comprises of the rugged stretch of mountainous country from Baluchistan to Kashmir, inhabited by tribes of Turko-Iranian origin who were made ferocious by nature of the land over whom civilization failed to exercise any softening influence. Thus the whole question of north-west frontier had two aspects, firstly, the protection and control of the passes which were like gates ; and secondly the subjugation and pacification of the tribal regions situated in the neighbouring east of these passes,

So far these aspects of the problem are concerned, they were not new, but at different periods of Indian history they assumed different shapes. During the periods when the lands in the east and the west of this region formed a part of the

---

*Revised from the paper "North-west frontier of the Sultanate during the thirteenth Century." first published in *The Indian Historial Quarterly*, Vol. xvii (1941), No. 1, pp. 59-69.

same kingdom the nature of the problem was simplified in as much as it was reduced to the question of merely keeping the line of communication open and keeping the tribal people satisfied and under control. But during the periods when different political authorities were set up on the two sides, this region played a vital role in determining the foreign policies of both the political powers. A strong and aggressive power established on the immediate vicinity of the frontier region always constituted a danger of supreme importance. It was this aspect of the problem that prompted Mahmud of Ghazna to annex the Punjab to his kingdom, and, later goaded Muhammad Ghuri to oust the Ghaznavides from the Punjab and establish his own authority over the entire region.

However, before we proceed with the examination of the question of the frontier under the Sultanate of Dehli, we may as well remember two geographical features of the Punjab of those days which to a greater measure determined the movements of the armies of the defending and the invading sides. They are : firstly, that the river beds of the Punjab were different from those of the present day,[1] secondly, that a regular route had developed between Dehli, Multan and Lahore. The route from Dehli to Bhatner (present Hanumangarh) was common, and passed through Rohtak, Hansi and Sirsa. At Bhatner the route bifurcated, one turned northwards and passing through Bhatinda, Muktesar and Kasur reached Lahore ; the other continued in the westerly direction along the bank of the river Ghaggar and to Uch via Marot, from Uch the route turned north and reached Multan. Multan and Lahore were also connected by means of another route.

To the Sultanate of Dehli the question of the frontier really came into being after the death of Shihabuddin Muhammad Ghuri when the Kingdom of Ghor disintegrated into fragments and India became an independent kingdom of the Turks. The Khwarizmian empire soon after annexed

---

1. Whitehead, R. B. 'The River courses of the Punjab and Sindh,' *Indian Antiquary*, 1932, pp. 163-69.

Ghazni and pushed its frontier upto the Indus.[2] The movement of the Khwarizmians, which was the result of the movement of the Mongols under Chingiz Khan, atonce became a danger to the infant Dehli Sultanate. It not only brought the Mongols on the borders of India,[3] but also cut off the Turks in India from their homeland there by deprived them of a land of retreat in case they were overwhelmed by the vast numbers of Indian population to whom the Turks were still foreigners. This situation dictated the internal and external policies of the Sultanate to a greater degree. However, for the present we are concerned with the policy and measures of the Sultans for meeting the situation at the north-west frontier.

The real change in the situation came with the ascendency of Chingiz Khan. Mongol out-posts were set up at Ghazni in the Peshawar valley and other places in Afghanistan. As a result of the Mongol activity the Indus could no longer remain as the political baundry. The frontier of the Dehli kingdom receded far into the interior of the Punjab.[4] The tract known as the Salt Range formed a part of the unregulated land inhabited by the hill tribes known as Khokhars. Awands and Janjuhas,[5] who, like some of the frontier tribes, were turbulent and were ever ready to defy any authority.

During the early years of conquest Lahore and Mu ltan were the westernmost provinces of Dehli. But Yalduz occupied Lahore on several occasions,[6] and for some time Lahore

---

2. Minahaj-us Siraj, *Tabqrt-i-Nasiri*, Eng. tr. Major H. G. Raverty, Bib. Ind. Series, 1881. Hence forth referred as Reverty. See, p. 267
3. Peshawar was the frontier outpost of Jalaluddin Khwarizm Shah when Chingiz Khan routed him in 1221 ; Raverty, pp. 285-93.
4. *ibid.*, p. 239, note 5.
5. *Shahpur Settlement Repot,* 1866, pp. 27, 28.
6. Raverty. pp. 526-30 and note 8 p. 526.

was equally claimed by Yalduz, Qubacha and Iltutmish.[7] Lahore occupied a strategic position from where the flanks of an army marching towards Multan could be easily destroyed, and, at the same time it formed a suitable base for any expedition in the unregulated tract of the Salt Range.

A brief survey of the situation on the borders of the kingdom of Iltutmish, at the very outset, will be useful in explaining the condition and its effect. The Khwarizmian prince Jalalud-din Mankbarni not daring to encounter the hostile forces of Chingiz Khan fled towards Indian frontier, though overtaken and defeated he managed to cross the Indus and entered Sind-Sagar Doab. Chingiz Khan remained on the other side of the river and engaged himself in reducing the Ighraki sect of the Khaljis who were allies of Jalalud-din and inhabited the northern regions of the river Kabul. Jalalud-din, having failed in his attempt to get shelter in the court of Iltutmish, turned towards Makhialah hills and from there sent his general with a small force that he had gathered round him to raid into the territory of the Khokhar chief. The chief Rai Sangin submitted to him and gave his daughter in marriage and sent his son with a force to assist him.[8] After thus buttressing his position Jalalud-din turned his attention towards the territories of Qubacha, which were in the west of the kingdom of Dehli. Jalalud-din's general Uzbak Pai with seven thousand horse attacked Qubacha's camp in the night and routed him.[9] Qubacha fled to Multan and readily complied with the demands of Jalalud-din which he fulfilled after reaching Uch.[10] The stay of Jalalud-din was not long. Ujbak Pai was left in charge of his Indian possessions and Saifud-din Hassan Qurlugh over his belongings of Ghazni while he left

7. *ibid.*, pp. 530-531.
8. Juwayni, Eng. Tr. The History of the World-Conqueror, Boyle, J. A. (1958), II, p. 414 ; *Indian Antiquary*, 1907, p. 3.
9. Juwayni, Eng. Tr., II, p. 414.
10. *ibid.*, p. 415.

lower Sindh by way of Mekran[11] in 621/1224. The effects of Jalalud-din's occupation and activities in the western Punjab were two-fold. It weakened Qubacha so as to be easily reduced by Iltutmish and, secondly, it exposed the boundry of the Sultanate to a heavy pressure of foreign raids.

At this period and some time after the frontier of the Sutanate extended to the Makhialah hills or the Salt Range.[12] It seems that Nandnah[13] was the fortress that commanded the frontier. Along with Nandanah, Kujah[14] was another fortress in the Salt Range forming the frontier, while Lahore was within the territory of Iltutmish. After the conquest of Lahore, Kujah and Nandanah had been placed under the charge of Malik Aitgin. The last expedition of Iltutmish in 633/1235 towards Baniyan[15] occupied by Saifud-din Hassan Qurlugh, and his activities against the hill tribes of the Salt Range were in fact his attempt to establish a frontier for his kingdom.

At the time of the death of Iltutmish the condition of the western frontier was no better than what it was when he had ascended the throne. The annexation of the dominions of Qubacha had brought the kingdom of Delhi directly in contact with the Mongol forees who were in occupation of the country west of the Indus. The situation became all the more worse because of the weak successors of Iltutmish and general disturbance caused by the court intrigues at Delhi.

During the reign of Ruknud-din Firuz in 634/1236 Saifuddin Hassan Qurlugh made his first attempt on the Lower Sindh and attacked Uch,[16] but he was repulsed and had to retrace his steps across the Indus. However, in

---

11. Raverty, p. 295 notes. :
12. *ibid.*, p. 609 and note 3.
13. *ibid.*, p., 534 n.
14. *ibid.*, p 629.
15. *ibid.*, pp. 623, n. 8, 536, n., 7 ; De, *Tab.-i-Akbari*, tr. I, p. 69 notes.
16. Raverty, pp. 683n6,730 and n. 7.

636/1238 when the Mongols captured Karman, Ghazni and Bamiyan he had to leave his original place and again come to India taking shelter in the Punjab.[17] Upto the year 1239 the river Chenab seems to have been the boundry line of the Delhi kingdom. We find, rebel noble Malik Kabir Khan retreating upto the river Chenab when pursued by the royal forces, but not daring to cross the river submitting to Sultan Raziya.[18] This indicates that the land beyrnd the Chenab was not under the jurisdiction of the Sultanate and Malik Kabir had no other alternative but to submit to the queen lest he should be overcome by the hostile Mongols.

In the year 639/1241-2, Bahadur Tair the commander of the Mongols of Herat, Ghor, Ghazni and Turkistan appeared before Lahore.[19] Malik Ikhtiyaruddin Quraqash Khan, the governor of the town finding himself unable to withstand the Mongol onslaught left the city and fell back towards Dehli. The city was completely destroyed and remained so till it was later restored by Balban. The Mongols, however, did not occupy the city for long, but after their evacuation the city was left exposed to the plunders of the Khokhars. Sometimes after the return of the Mongols. Qaraqash Khan no doubt drove the Khokhars out of the vicinity of Lahore, but he could not restore the city to its former condition. The frontier tract because of Mongol invasions, was in a state of utmost political confusion. In the north the hill tribes were prctically independent and used to take advantage of the defeat of either party. The Khokhars, Awands and Janjuhas occupaid the northern portion of the Sindh-Sagar Doab, and the Khokhars were gradually during this period spreading even beyond the river Beas, and formed a part of the army of Raziya[20]

The province of Lahore with its dependency was, however, reorganised during the reigh of Alaud-din Masaud Shah

17. *ibid.*, p. 1129.
18. *ibid.*, p. 727.
19. *ibid* , pp. 1129-32
20. *ibid*, p. 647,n9.

and was placed under Malik Ikhtiyar-uddin Yuzbak-i-Tughril Khan.[21] Thus Lahore became the frontier out-post of the Sultanate from where the frontiers were to be guarded.[22] Thus the boundry line of the Dehli Sutanate had receded and the river Ravi roughly formed the outer line of the frontier province. The boundry line had receded in Sindha as well. Malik Kabir Khan, who had been appointed as Muqta of Multan by Sultan Raziya, asserted his independence in 639/1241-42 when Bahadur Tair invaded Lohore. He also occupied Uch and Lower Sindh.[23] Through Malik Kabir Khan died within the year of asserting independence his son Tajud-din Abu Baqr continued the independence of his house and several times repulsed the attacks of Hassan Quarlugh on Multan.[24] Uch had been placed under the charge of Mukhl-is-ud-din, a *Khawajasara* of Tajud-din Abu Baqr, who kept the place well defended. But Malik Kabir Khan's dynasty soon came to an end with the death of Tajud-din Abu Baqr. In the absence of his master, Mukhlis-ud-din could not hold his ground for long and completely collapsed when the Mongols under Mangutah invested Uch in 643/1245. The citizens finding themselves in a precarious condition appealed for help to Dehli. Ulugh Khan was sent with the imperial forces and on his arrival the Mongols withdrew from Uch.[25] As a result of this movement the authority of Dehli Sultan was reestablished in Sindh. After making necessary arrangements at Uch and Multan, Ulugh Khan proceeded to chastise the hill tribes of Jud. But the disturbance and deposition of Masaud Shah at Dehli led him to hasten to the capital and he could hardly achieve any thing in region It seems that Ulugh Khan attempted at recovering Nandanah during this movement as he directed several raids in the Salt range. But the tract beyond the Ravi could not be recovered for the time

21. *ibib.*, p. 762.
22. *ibid.*, p. 657.
23. *ibid.*, p. 727.
24. *ibid.*
25. *ibid.*, pp. 809-10.

being and it rema.ned more or less in condition that might be called as the Mongol sphare of influence.

During the year 644/1246 the Mongols invaded Lahore and the governor not finding himself capable of resisting them offered a ransom of 30,000 *dirhams*, 30 kharwars of soft goods and 100 heads of captives.[26] After this Lahore too seems to have gone outside the jurisdiction of Dehli at least upto 652/1254. In 646/1249 Hassan Qurlvgh again appeared before the walls of Multan then held by Malik Kashlu Khan. The Malik hastened from Uch and through Hassan Qurlugh was killed in action, Kashlu Khan could not hold the place and had to evacuate it.[27] In the mean time Sher Khan who had been appointed Muqta of Bhatinda occupied Multan and placed it under his own officer Malik Ikhtiyar-un-din Kurez[28]. Sher Khan also attacked Uch and drove away Kashlu Khan from there in 1250-51. But on account of the ascendency of the non-Turkish nobles at the capital in 1253 headed by Imadud-din Riyahan his possessions in Sindh were Transfered to Arslan Khan.[29] Sher Khan, thereupon, retired to Turkistan and went to the court of Mangu Khan.[30]

In 646/1248 Sultan Nasirud-din Mahmud, while returning from Kara, granted the iqta of Sambhal and Badayun to his brother Jalalud-din, but on reaching his new assignment the prince became apprehensive of his position and without waiting proceeded towards Lahore by way of Sirmur hills.[31] The cause of Jalalud-din's fear has not been mentioned by Minhaj, but the manner in which he narrates the incident suggests that in all likelihood Jalaud-din was afraid of the

26. *ibid.*, pp. 677 n6, 1201 notes.
27. *ibid.*, p. 782
28. *ibid.*, p. 792.
29. *ibid.*, p. 695.
30. *ibid.*, pp. 695, 792 notes, 1225 notes. Raverty mentions that the arrival of SherKhan at the Mongol court in 1254 in mentioned by the Christian missionary Rubruquis.
31. *ibid.*, p. 684 and notes.

growing power of Balban and suspected some foul play on his part. While dealing with the biography of Balban, Minahaj mentions that "in the month of Shaban, 646 H., the royal standards moved towards the upper provinces as far as the extreme confines, and the bank of the river Biah, and from thence returned again to the capital."[32] This movement of the Dehli troops could not have been but connected with the pursuit of the flight of Prince Jalalud-din. This passage also indicates that the boundry of Dehli kingdom extended only upto the river Beas. The fugitive prince Jalud-din went to the court of Mangu Khan and sought his help and finally returned to the Punjab with Sali Bahadur and others[33] some time in 651/1253. Jalud-din seems to have subsequently held Lahore under Mongol protection. No doubt he joined the Turkish nobles against the Riyhanis and appearing from the side of Lahore joined their camp at Bhatinda[34] and some reconciliation was also brought about between him and Sultan Nasirud-din[53] but he remained in Lahore independent of the Dehli authority. Thus Lahore remained outside the jurisdiction of the Sultanate of Dehli.

The north west frontier boundary of the Delhi Sultanate thus had receded from the Ravi to the river Beas which was now accepted as the boundry with Bhatinda as the frontier out post.[36]

After the victory of the Turkish party over the Riyhanis, Malik Sher Khan was given the province of Bhatinda to

32. *ibid.*, p. 818.
33. *Wassaf* (Elliot, iii, pp. 37,38)
34. Raverty, p. 830, notes 4, 5.
35. *ibid.*, p. 700.
36. Beas flowing in its old bed before the Sutlej joined it from the east. See, R. B Whitehead, 'River courses of the Punjab and Sind', *Indian Antiquary*, 1932, pp. 168-69 ; R. D. Oldham, 'On the probable changes in the geography of the Punjab and its rivers', *Journal Asiatic Society of Bengal*, 1886, pp. 322-43

guard the frontiers. This change in the frontier led to serious Mongol menace who now were free to move in the Punjab.[37] The Mongol preasure became so acute that the Mewati trouble in 658/1260 could not be subdued. This was the period when the policy of the Sultante in the frontier region was at its worst. Both Lahore and Sindh at this time were outside the jurisdiction of the Dehli Sultanate. Sindh was held by Kashlu Khan as a protege of the Mongols[38] and the Dehli Sultan being afraid of incurring the displeasure of the Mongols transferred Sher Khan from Bhatinda to Koil, Gwalior and other places. Sher Khan was hostile towards Kashlu Khan and this transfer was aimed at avoiding any clash on the frontier[39] in which the Mongols might be involved. Sher Khan was replaced by Malik Nasrat Khan who was given the charge of Bhatinda, Sunam, Samana and Lakhawal and the frontiers as far as the ferries over the river Beas.[40]

During the period of his naibship, Balban gradually developed a policy for solving the frontier problem. While he did not disturb Kashlu Khan all at once, he launched upon the policy of establishing friendly relations with the Mongols. He tried to marry one of his sons to a grand-daughter of Hassan Qurlugh and sent Jamalud-din Khalji as envoy for this purpose.[41] The envoy was well received by Hulagu who in exchange sent his own envoy to the court of Dehli. The envoy of Halagu reached Dehli in 658/1260 and Balban arranged a magnificient reception for the Il Khanid envoy. Minhaj remarks, "when the emissaries reached the capital the sovereign of Islam, in requital and return for that honour which Hulagu, the Mughal had been pleased to show towards the the Hajib of the court... great favour was lavished upon his emissaries likewise."[42] The exchange of envoys had the

37. Raverty, pp. 850-51.
38. *ibid.*, pp. 784 & notes, L.
39. *ibid.*, p. 794.
40. *ibid.*, p. 788 & notes.
41. *ibid*, pp. 860-62.
42. *ibid*, p. 863.

desired effect, and we are informed that Hulagu Khan issued orders to his officers posted on the Indian frontier to respect the boundry of the Dehli Sultanate.[43]

The friendly attitute of Hulagu Khan brought about comparative peace on the Sindh-Multan border and the Mongol raids from the Il Khanid branch of the Mongols ceased for some time. Halugu's son and successor Abaga (1265-81) continued the policy of his father. Another effect of this policy was that Kashlu Khan who was holding Multan and Sindh as a protege of the Il Khanids was contained witnin his own limits without causing trouble to the Dehli kingdom. The Mongols during this period were divided into several groups and were constantly at war with each other. The regions of Trans-Oxiana with Afghanistan and the regions adjacent to the Khybar were under the Chagtais who were not on friendly terms with the Il Khanids. Thus friendly relations with the Il Khanids could not prevent the Chagtais from raiding Indian territories in the Punjab.

To meet the Mongol raids Balban posted Sher Khan on the Punjab frontier. He was given the charge of Sunam, Bhatinda, Lahore and Dipalpur Sher Khan rebuilt the fortress of Bhatner and maintained a well equipped army of several thousand horsemen, and, by suppressing the Jats, Khokhars, Mandahirs along with the Bhattis who inhabited the unregulated regions, he restored some order and control.[44] From his charge in the frontier region Sher Khan effectively checked the Mongols from entering the Sultanate territory.

Early in his reign Balban led an expedition into the Salt Range and two years later he proceeded to Lahore, re-built and re-populated it and made fresh appointment of officers for its administration.[45] But Lahore could not regain its import-

---

43. *ibid.*, pp. 862-63.
44. Ziaud-din Barani, *Tarikh--Firuzshahi,* Bib. Ind. Text. [Henceforth referred as Barani] p. 65.
45. Barani, pp. 60, 70.

ance as frontier outpost. Dipalpur now was recognised as the real outpost with the head quarters of the person incharge of the Punjab frontier.

In Sindh-Multan region Kashlu Khan could not remain for long. We have no precise account to enable us state definitely the process through which Kashlu Khan was ousted from Multan. Isami no doubt tells us a story which is quite interesting but of doubtful verasity. According to Isami's version Balban forced Kashlu Khan to evacuate Multan. But it seems that after Balban's accession, Kashlu Khan finding no support from the Il Khanids where the new Il Khan Abaga was in no mood to enter into hostility with the Sultan of Dehli withdrew support and Kashlu Khan not being on friendly terms with Balban and also being afraid of Balban's policy of liquidating the Chahalgani left Multan sometime after the death of Sher Khan, who it was rumoured had been poisoned by Balban,[46] and retired into Bamiyan. After the exit of Kashulu Khan and Sher Khan Sultan Balban took some positive steps to meet the situation at the frontier. He divided the whole frontier into two sections *i.e.* the Punjab frontier and the Sindh-Multan frontier. This measure most probably was taken in the sixth year of his reign. It was after the death of Sher Khan, which took place in the fourth or the fifth year of his reign, we are told that Balban sent his eldest son Prince Muhammad to Take charge of the Multan frontier.[47] After the death of Sher Khan the Punjab frontier was divided into several charges. Samana and Sunam were placed under Timur Khan, a member of the Chahalgani, and other officers were placed at different outposts but all of them failed to achieve the results that had been obtained by Sher Khan. The pressure of the Chagatai Mongol attack continued on the Punjab border which at times acquired menacing shape.

---

46. *ibid.*, p. 66.

47. *ibid.*

Some time after the death of Sher Khan and after the failure of his officers Balban appointed his second son Prince Bughra Khan as the warden of the frontier with Sunam and Samana as important outposts. The river Beas at this time seems to have been the accepted boundary of the Sultanate. During this period whenever the Mongol raids are mentioned, it is said that the royal forces obtained victories and drove away the enemies so that they were unable to advance beyond the Beas.[48] Thus it is clear that the real hold of the Dehli Sultanate during this period was upto the Beas and any attempt at further encroachment or advance beyond the river was effectively checked. We can therefore, safely conclude that the Beas formed the boundary in the Punjab frontier with extension upto Lahore. To guard this frontier region Balban constructed new forts ond ordered for the repair of the old ones. He garrisoned these forts with experienced soldiers and efficient generals. He also attached some land to these forts the produce of which was to be stored in the forts so as to enable them to stand any siege that may result from Mongol incursions. In the Multan frontier the matters were comparatively better under the able generalship of Prince Muhammad.

The situation in Persia, however, changed in 1281 when Abaga died and his younger brother Tagudar occupied the throne by passing Arghun the eldest son of Abaga. Arghun raised the standard of rebellion against his uncle, and though he was defeated and imprisoned his life was spared. But soon after the Mongol generals resented Tagudars conversion to Islam and his assumption of the name Ahmad. They took up the cause of Arghun and rescued him from prison. In the general uprising that followed Tagudar (Ahmad) was overthrown and put to death in 1284. The accession of Arghun, however, did not bring peace and order atonce in the Il chanid territory. This change in the situation seriously effeeted the Indian frontier as the Mongols in their effort to replenish their resources started raiding Indian territories.

48. *ibid.*, p. 81.

It was in this process that in 1285 Samar Khan, a Mongol general came with a force towards India.[49]

In the battle with Samar Khan Prince Muhammad was slain and Amir Khusrau was taken away as captive. After the death of Prince Muhammad (*Khan-i-Shahid*) Balban gave the charge of the frontier province of Sindh with Multan to Kai Khusrau.[50] In making this appointment, Balban seems to have been guided more by his family or dynastic considerations than by the principle of efficiency. The young prince was certainly no match to the task entrusted to him. But Kai Khusrau continued at Multan till he fell to the conspiracy of Nizamud-din in the reign of Kaiqubad and was murdered in the town of Rohtak.[51] During the weak reign of Kaiqubad the frontier region seems to have been neglected and Sindh remained in a disturbed state. Kaiqubad's move to sent Nizamuddin to Multan to look after the frontier proved abortive as the latter declined to leave the capital and the Sultan found himself absolutely in the clutches of the ambitious noble Nizamuddin.

In the region of the Punjab frontier, Jalulud-din Khalji was posted sometimes after the transfer of Bughra Khan to Bengal and remained there till the last year of Kaiqubad's reign. Amir Khusrau in his *Qiranus Sadain* mentions that when Tamur Khan led the Mongols and over ran the bank of the Ravi extending from Lahore to Multan[52] Malik Bektars was sent with a force of three thousand and routed the Mongols on the bank of the Ravi and made large number of prisoners.[53] This passage evidently refers to the early years of the short reign of Kaiqubad. We know that Jalaud-din Khalji was posted on the frontier where he showed his mettle as a soldier and as the warden of the marches he remained at

49. Barani, p. 109.
50. *ibid.*, p. 110.
51. *ibid.*, p. 133.
52. Amir Khusrau, *Qiranus Sadain*, p. 49.
53. *ibid.*, p. 50 ; *Tarkih-i-Mubarakshahi*, p. 54.

Samana and Sunam and controled Dipalpur. It was from this region that he came to Dehli towards the later years of Kaiqubad's reign. Thus Sunam and Samana remained as the frontier provinces wlth the western boundary roughly corresponding with the river Beas, and Dipalpur on the bank of the Beas had become the seat of the 'warden of the marches'

Thus the north-west-frontier except for a brief period of the reign of Iltutmish remained between the rivers Ravi and the Beas throughout the so-called Slave dynasty ; and the watershed of the two rivers roughly formed the boundary line of the empire, with the utmost expansion upto the left bank of the Ravi in certain periods. While the river Beas was within their territory the river Ravi was not. Whenever the Mongols crossed the Beas or attempted to cross, the Imperial army or the Governor in charge pursued them crossing the river but they hardly ever crossed the river Ravi in the pursuit of the enemy. Lahore on the left bank of the Ravi occupied an inportant though isolated position in the region. Samana, Sunam, Dipalpur, Lahore etc. were then frontier divisions and none of them are situated beyond the Ravi Thus it is erroneous to assert the Indus river as the frontier boundary of the Dehli Sultanate in the thirteenth century. The river Indus in the Punjab was far outside the jurisdiction of the Sultanate.

The so-called Slave rulers were never able to achieve a natural frontier from where they could ward off the foreign invaders *i. e.* the Mongols. The western Punjab was either in a no mans land or was within the Mongol sphere of influence. Western Punjab being outside the pale of the Sultanate the Slave rulers with all their precaution could not prevent the Mongols from entering into their territory and from becoming a menace to them. It is in this absence of a natuaral frontier that we get an answer to the failure of the Sultans in checking the Mongol attacks and their march at times right upto Dehli in spite of the fact that the Mongols were never strong enough either to defeat the Sultan or to stay in India.

B. Under the Khalji Turks

The north-west frontier of the Ilbari Turks or the Memluk sultans had remained between the rivers Ravi and the Beas and the water parting line of the two rivers had roughly formed the boundary line in the north-west, albeit with brief intervals when their territory stretched beyond the river Ravi. For the protection of this frontier, Multan, Samana, Sunam, Dipalpur and Lahore served as military outposts. The fall of the Ilbari Turks brought the Khalji Turks into power. The Khaljis have been characterised as imperialists. They conquered almost the whole of the south and at the same time consolidated their rule in the Hindustan. But in the region of north-west they did not achieve the natural frontier of India, nor did they follow a po'icy for its achievment.

The Khalji era began with the accession of Jalaluddin Firuz Khalji on 3rd Jamada II 689 H[1] (June 13, 1290 A. D.). Jalaluddin had served on the frontiers. He had established his leadership of the Khaljis, and his reputation as a soldier, by his military exploits against the Mongols. But on his assumption of sovereignty he merely continued the frontier policy of his predecessors. The discourse between Sultan Jalaluddin and Ahmad Chap throws a good deal of light on the affairs of the frontier. The Sultan's reply to Ahmad Chap that he would go to Multan and like Sher Khan (Sunqar) fight against the Mongols and make them incapable of entering Muslim territory[2], clearly indicates that Multan was the frontier and the territory beyond Multan did not belong to the Dehli Sultanate. In other words the political boundary of the Sultanate in the north-west continued as it had been under the Ilbaris.

Sultan Jalaluddin Khalji observed a peace policy on the frontier and completely failed to understand the importance of frontier defence. In the year 691 H/1291-92 A. D. when

1. Amir Khurau, *Miftiahulfutuh* (Aligarh) p. 7.
2. Barani (*Tarikh-i-Firuz Shahi,* Bib Ind. Text) p. 187. Henceforth referred in as *Barani.*

Abdullah[3] a grandson of Hulaqu Khan of Persia invaded India, the Sultan concluded a treaty with him. The 'IlKhans of Persia from the time of Arghun (D. 1921) were following an aggressive policy towards India, but were always checked on the Multan frontier. The death of Arghun was followed by the usual scramble for power amongst the members of the house. It was during this disturbance that Abdullah had turned towards India, with a view to improve his material resources.

Abdullah had marched upto Barram[4], where the vanguard of the sultan's army also reached. The two armies pitched their camps with the river between them. A number of skirmishes took place between the two vangnards and through contemporary Indian chroniclers would have us believe that the forces of Delhi Sultan won a great victory over the Mongols, the subsequent treaty clearly indicates that at best there could have been only some skirmishes. Sultan Jalaluddin and Abdullan conferred at a meeting and a treaty was concluded[5]. The Sultan addressed Abdullah as his son. Ulghu Khan, another member of the house of Chingiz, along with some 4,000[6] followers as well as their families opted to stay in India. The Sultan gave one of his daughters in marriage to Ulghu Khan.[7] The soldiers of the two sides sold and purchased commodities and also exchanged presents.

From the above summary of events of the year 691 H/ 1291-92 A. D. we find that Sultan Jalaluddin thought of pro-

---

3. *Barani*, p 218.
4. See Lal, (*History of the Khaljis*) p. 37 fn. 76 ; Badayuni has Sanam (Ranking) Vol. I. p. 236 ; Sanam or Sunam could not have been on the River Sindh, it could be any place near Samana as found from the readings of *Tabaqat-i-Nasiri*, p. 219 ; *Firishta*, I, p. 72 ; *Barani*, pp. 80. 85
5. *Barani*. p. 219, mentions Ulghu Khan as a grandson of Chingiz Khan.
6. *Firishta*, I, p, 94, gives this number.
7. *Barani*, p. 219.

tecting his kingdom from the attack of the Mongols through a conciliatory policy and also by offering them an assylum in India. Such a policy towards the IlKhan branch of Mongols could work out succesfully but the Sultan seems to have been quite ignorant of the struggle that was going on amongst the descendants of Chingiz Khan At a result of this struggle quite a large number of them had lost their homeland, and partly for this reason so many Mongols decided to stay in India, It is also significant that Multan frontier was well protected. What about the frontier-lying between the Punjab and Afghanistan ? Did the Sultan ever think of it ? The narratives of the various chronicles only lead to the conclusion that the Sultan never thought of it. Thus on the Lahore side the river Ravi continued as the boundry of the Sultanate and remained exposed to the Mongol raids, which grew into menacing dimension about five or six years later.

Sultan 'Alauddin ascended the throne of Dehli in 695/1296 A. D. after murdering Sultan Jalaluddin and had to bear the brunt of Mongol invasions for about a decade. The cause of these raids lay primarily in the political conditions prevailing outside the borders of India, particularly in Central Asia. Dava, a descendant of Chaghtai, in alliance with Qaidu, had started a struggle against the IlKhan of Persia in the west and the Great Khan in the east. Qaidu was a descendant of Oqtai, the third son of Chingiz Khan and his successors as the Great Khan. The house of Oqtai had been ousted from the Khanate by Mangu Khan son of Tuli. Halaqu Khan another son of Tuli had established himself in Persia and his descendants were known as 'IlKhans. Mangu Khan was succeeded by his son Qublai Khan as the Great Khan. Thus the Great Khan and the IlKhan being deseendants of Tuli formed one group. Qaidu, son of Kuyuk who had been ousted from the Khanate by Mangu Khan, considered the Great Khan as usurper and was making effort to wrest the Khanate from him. Dava had a special grudge against Qublai Khan, because of his interference in Transoxiana, a territory given to Chaghtai by Chingiz Khan. Qublai Khan had appointed Mubarak Shah over Transoxiana, which had resulted in a contest between Dava's father Borak and Mubarak Shah. Dava had thus inherited from his father the contest against the Great Khan who in his turn, had secured the loyalty of the 'Ilkhans of Persia. Dava had thus to fight hard on both the sides of his kingdom of Transoxiana. He had gained an initial success in Ghazni and thus was posted right across the botders of India It was in the course of this life and death struggle that whenever hard pressed Dava sent expedition to India in search of resources, both men and money. Besides, whenever his men lost some ground they thought of crossing the borders and coming to India.

The first Mongol raid in the reign of 'Alauddin Khalji took place in 696 H/1296 A.D. i.e. practically within the year of his accession. The leader of this invasion was Kadar Khan[8] a 'General' of Dava, who after crossing the Indus started by rapid marches towards the kingdom of Dehli from a northernly direction. Ulugh Khan and Zafar Khan were sent from Dehli who met the advancing armies of the Mongols in the vicinity of Jari Manjaur[9].

---

8. *Khazainul Futuh* (Eng. Tr. Habib) p 23.
9. *Knazainul Futuh* (Eng. Tr, Habib), 23 ; *Tab-i-Akbari*, I, p. 141 has Jaranmahmur ; *Badauni* (Tr.) I. p 249, has Manjahur ; *Cambridge History of India*, Vol, III, p. 100 says Jullundhar ; *Barani* (Bib, Ind. Text) has Jullundhar. But *Elliot* Vol. III p. 162 has pointed out "So (Julludhar) in the print but the MSS have Jadwa O Manjaur and Jarat Mahud."

   Manjha in the Lahore Dittrict seems to be the place referred by the chroniclers, because of its geographical situation fitting closely with their descriptions *Imperial Gazrtters of India*, Vol. XVII, p, 196, describe Manjha as follows :—"A tract of country in the Lahore and Amritsar districts of the Punjab lying between 30 . 52° N and 21.35 N [*obviously a mis-print*] and 73·45 E and 75 21 E and forming a portion of uplands of Bari Doab. In

(*Contd. on next page*)

Amir Khusrau has clearly mentioned that the field of battle was Jaran Manjaur. A reading of the contemporary chroniclers clearly indicates that this battle took place in the Bari Doab. We are not told anywhere that after the defeat of the Mongols they were chased to lands beyond Bari Doab. This leads to the conclusion that beyond the Bari Doab was a land where it was useless to chase the Mongols or more clearly that beyond this land was foreign territory. Thus we find that at the beginning of his reign 'Alauddin's frontier on the Punjab side extended upto the Bari Doab. Now it remains to examine whether at any stage of his reign more territories were conquered on this side or if ever any attempt was made by the Sultan for his purpose. In the absence of any definite mention of his territorial limits in this direction by the chroniclers we are left only with the deductions to be drawn from the descriptions of the various Mongol invasions.

Next invasion of the Mongols took place in the third year of 'Alauddin's reign[10] when Ulugh Khan and Nusarat Khan

---

(*Contd. from previous page*)

shape it is roughtly speaking a triangle whose base may be taken as the Grand Trunk road crossing the Ravi to the Beas and whose sides on the high banks marking the ancient courses of these river. From the point where the Beas now joins the Sutlej the old Beas bank diverges from the present course of the Sutlej and approaches the old bed of the Ravi near the border of Motgomery Distt, This is the appex of Manjha."

Tarikh-i-Mubarakshahi, Tex. p. 218 : Yahiya has again mentioned Jaran Manjhur in connection with the raid of Sheikh Ali in the reign of Mubarak Shah Saiyid.

Prof. Basu (Tr. p, 226 n 4 and 5) identifies Jaran with Zira in Ferozepur Distt. 33° 58' N, 75° 2' 45" E and Manjahur with Makhu in the same Dist. 31°. 6' N, 75° 5' E.

10. *Barani,* p. 253.

were sent to Gujarat. Mongols under Saldi[11] came upto the north western part of Sindh and occupied the fort of Siwistan (or Sahwan), Zafar Khan successfully defected them and drove them out of the place and captured their leader. The most striking point in this raid of the Mongols is, that the Government of Delhi and the officers of the frontier outpost of Multan could only learn about the movement of the Mongols when they had occupied Sehwan. This leads to the inference that lands in the regions beyond the frontier mentioned above being outside the territories of the Sultan, there was no means of getting information of their movements.

Saldi's invasion was followed by another within the same year[12] under the leadership of Qutlugh Khwajah, with him Targhi had also come. These Mongol leaders caught 'Alauddin napping and completely engulfed in his dreams of world conquest and of founding a new religion. The Mongols had reached Kili in the neighbourhood of Siri, the Khalji capital, and created such terror in the minds of the people which can easily be understood through the garbled language of Barani saying that the Kotwal suggested bribing of the Mongols. However, 'Alauddin retained his honour as a soldier and a general by giving battle to them and also gaining a victory though at the cost of the life of Hizbruddin Zafar Khan[13]. After defeating the Mongols the question comes, how far did the Imperial forces pursue the Mongols. We do not find any mention of the Imperial forces having pursued the fugitives into lands mentioned above as outside the kingdom i.e. lands beyond the Ravi.

---

11. *Barani*, p. 253 ; *Tab-i-Akbari* p. 142 ; *Badayuni* Tr., I, p. 249 ; *Firishta*, I, p. 103 ; *Isami* (Agra Edition), p. 241, All agree about the leader : Badayuni has confused this invasion with the first Mongol invasion and says Saldi was defeated at Jarin Manjur. Yahiya has not mentioned about this invasion.
12. *Barani*, p. 254.
13. *ibid.*, p. 260 ; *'Isami* pp. 246-60 ; *Zafarul Walih*, p. 797.

The Mongols again appeared in 703/1303 A. D. under the leadersdip of Targhi, when 'Alauddin had just returned after his conquest of Chittor. The Mongols this time, instead of wasting their time in devastation of lands on their route, had quickly marched upto Delhi and besieged the capital. According to Barani[14], "the siege was so complete and effective that 'Alauddin could get no help from outside. The army that was returning from Warangal under Malik Fakhruddin was completely exhausted and could not break through the cordon of Mongol siege. Even the army at Samana, Sunam, Dipalpur and Multan was not in a position to give succur to 'Alauddin. If Targhi had remained for some more time there might have been a general panic and Delhi might have been lost[15]. Mongols obviously had no knowledge of successfully concluding a seige. They could fight on the open field, but on this particular occasion they never got the chance and were self exhausted while waiting for a decisive encounter, thus Targhi returned towards his own country.

After the attack of Targhi, 'Alauddin took measures for frontier defence. These measures included orders for repair of old forts lying on the route of the Mongols. These forts were required to equip themselves with war engine like *'manjniks'* and *'aradas* ; they were provided with skilled workers, and arrangement for storing grain and fodder was also made. Besides, Dipalpur and Samana were ordered to be garrisoned with strong and selected forces and to remain

---

14. *Barani*, pp. 300-302.
15. This is how Barani has expressed the severity of the siege, and says that by the mercy of God the Mongols were unable to find any means of forcing the Camp and overpowering the Royal Army. After two months the prayers of the wretched prevailed and the accursed Targhi retreated towards his own country ; Yahiya says that Malik Fakhruddin and Malik Tughlaq made a night attack and defeating the mongols captured Targhi, *Tarikh-i-Mubarak Shahi* (Tr.) p. 71 ; *Isami*, p. 277.

in vigilance. The *iqta's* on the routes of the Mongols were placed under experienced *amirs* and whole route was secured by the appointment of tried and vigilant generals.[16]

Before 'Alauddin's measures could take shape, the Mongols in 703H/1304 A. D. under the leadership of 'Ali Beg and Tartaq[17] proceeded along the foot of Sirmur hills to the bank of the Beas, and while a portion of their army harried Nagore, the main army marched to Doab, between the Ganges and the Jamuna[18]. This invasion too like the previous ones was easily checked. Malik Kafur and Ghazi Malik led the forces of the Delhi kingdom and defeating the Mongols captured a large number of them. It is worth nothing that in this expedition too, the Imperial forces did not pursue the fugitive Mongols for a longer distance, and that the chroniclers have mentioned the river Beas as one that was involved.

The Mongols next appeared under the leadership of Kank or Gung and invaded the region of Khekar on the Ghaggar (or Patiala region on Ghaggar)[19]. Malik Kafur and Ghazi Malik were again sent against the Mongols. These two generals took up a position near the Ravi on the route by which the Mongols were expected to return. Their calculations proved correct and the Mongols while returning were surprised and defeated and their leader Kank was captured and sent as a prisoner to Delhi. This invasion of Kank was followed next year by another raid towards the region of Siwalik hills, and Malik Kafur and Ghazi Malik again followed the same tactics, and awaiting on the banks of the Ravi captured a large number of them.

By now 'Alauddin's administrative measures must have taken a definite shape and form· On the frontier region Ghazi Malik was appointed as the warden of the marches

16. *Barani* pp 302-303.
17. *Khazain-ul-Futuh* (Tr.), p. 26 : Amir Khusrau mentions Targhi also among the leaders.
18. *Tarikh-i-Mubarak Shahi* (Tr.), p. 71.
19. *Tab-i-Akbari* (Tr.), I, p. 179, fn. 2.

with his headquarters at Dipalpur with Lahore as an appanage. Ghazi Malik remained as the 'Warden' of the marches till the end of the Khalji rule. After his appointment at Dipalpur the Mongols again appeared in 1307-8 A.D. under the leadership of Iqbal Mandah. The Mongols were again defeated and the captives were sent to Delhi. After this invasion Mongols practically ceased to come to India. Ghazi Malik adopted different tactics. Instead of waiting for the Mongols he would advance every winter upto the Mongol frontier and challenge them for engagement. The Mongols of course never accepted this challenge. Thus Ghazi Malik remained a great bulwark against the advance of the Mongols in the districts of Dipalpur and Lahore[20]. This brings in the question of Mongol frontier. The answer to this question can be found in the appeal of Ghazi Malik to the nobles when he tried to organise them against the usurption of the throne of Delhi by Nasiruddin Khusrau Shah[21]. While we are informed that he appealed to nobles of Multan and Siwistan we do not find him seeking help of any noble from lands beyond Lahore. This further lends support to the conclusion that lands beyond the river Ravi did not belong to the kingdom of Delhi and hence the frontier outpost of Dipalpur and Lahore served the purpose of guarding the frontiers.

Thus we find that the rivers Sutlej, Beas and Ravi were inside the territories of the Khalji empire and the lands beyond the Ravi on the Lahore frontier were outside the kingdom, and that Dipalpur, Samna, Sunam, Lahore and Multnn were most important strategic frontier outposts of which Dipalpur was considered as the most important outpost, with the headquarters of the "Warden" of the marches. The western boundary of the Khalji Empire can therefore be

20. *Barani*, pp. 322, 323 ; *Tab-i-Akbari* (Tr.), 180.
21. *Barani*, p. 416 ; *Tarikh-i-Mubarak Shani* (Tr.) p. 89 ; *Tab-i-Akbari* (Tr.) p. 205 ; *Tughlaqnamah*, pp. 63-70 ; 'Isami (pp. 369, 372, 375) however, mentions the name of Gulchand and Shijari the Khokar chiefs who also joined Malik Tughlaq on this occasion.

roughly formed by joining the eastern slopes of Kirthar Range to Sibi and thence to Multan, from Multan along the river to the junction of the Ravi with the combined waters of the Chenab and the Jhelum and thence along the river Ravi to the foot of the hills and this boundary remained upto the end of the Khalji rule. Beyond this line the territories were either under the control of the Mongols or were under the Mongol sphere of influence, and directly under the control of the Ghakkars and the Khokars[22].

It was this absence of natural frontier of the Empire of Delhi under the Khaljis that rendered possible the constant raids of Mongols, the genesis of which lay in the disturbed condition prevailing in Transoxiana. Any statesman with some farsight could have easily realised the situalion of the north-west frontier. But Sultan 'Alauddin took no measures to secure the natural frontier of India, while he was sending expeditions to the far south for conquest, the idea of the natural frontier never struck him.

---

22. I find it difficult to agree with Dr. K. S. Lal (*History of Khaljis*, pp. 175, 176) that Alauddin's Khutba was read at Ghazni or that Malik Ghazi i.e. Ghiyasuddin raided Ghazni, because of the following reasons :—

    (i) No army from the centre was sent to help Ghazi Malik to march to Ghazni and his personal contingent at Dipalpur could not have been large enough for such a hazard particularly when he did not dare to march against Khusrau Shah unaided by other Maliks.

    (ii) Amir Khusrau would certainly have mentioned it in *Tughlaq Nama*.

    (iii) Barani certainly would have mentioned it with great applause.

    Thus the letter as referred in *Elliot* III p. 566-67, needs further examination before it can be taken as a positive evidence.

The much praised economic and military reforms of 'Alauddin may have strengthened his hold on the country but the frontier of this big empire ever remained exposed to foreign aggression. The absence of the Mongol raids towards the later periods of his reign, was not due to his reforms but because of the altered situation in Transoxiana following the the death of Dava in 1307 A.D.

After the death of Qaidu in 1301 Dava was maintaining law and order and preventing the clash of arms amongst the membecs of Oqtai and Chaghtai clans upto 1307 A.D. But his death deprived the Chaghtais of his wise counsel. The members of the Oqtai and Chaghtai houses started fighting amongst themselves. The whole of Transoxiana was torn to pieces, which the best efforts of Kebek and Tarmashirin, the sons of Dava, failed to restore.

On the Multan frontier the friendly relations with the 'IlKhans, established by Jalaluddin Khalji, coutinued under two successive rules i.e. Ghazan Khan (1295-1304)[23] and Aljaitu (1301-16). Khwaja Rashiduddin came to India as an envoy of 'IlKhans Ghazan Khan and was well received by 'Alauddin Khalji. The Sultan even relaxed his anti-liquor policy and the Khwaja was served with wine. The Sultan granted *'Jogir'* to the Khwaja and instructed revenue officers that the income from the *'Jagir'* be properly transmitted to to the Khwaja through traders. Thus it is clear that Sultan 'Alauddin was anxious to keep up the friendship with the IlKhans of Persia, but if he had expected to use the 'IlKhans as a buttress against the Chaghtais and Oqtais he was in the wrong. The Chaghtais were in possession of territories before which the north west frontier of India stood most vulnerable.

Thus we see that the affairs of the North-West Frontier region of the Khalji Sultans in general and 'Alauddin Khalji

23. Barthold, *Turkistan Down to the Mongol Invasion*, (Eng. Tr, Second Edition, 1928), p. 44.

in particular did not improve beyond what was left by the 'Memluk' Sultans. With the river Ravi as their frontier line the entire westen Punjab remained outside their territory. The frontier forts such as Multan, Dipalpur, Lahore and Samana while serving as strong defence outposts, could never control the frontier passes such as Khyber or Bolan from where foreign aggression could have been more effectively checked. The western Punjab being outside the pale of Khalji Empire, 'Alauddin could not prevent the Mongols from becoming a menace to his subjects. So far as the policy is concerned we find that 'Alauddin's genius in this particalar aspect could not conceive of anything better than raising an army and strengthening the outposts. A real national monarch or statesman should have thought of the natural frontier for the big empire he was creating, but 'Alauddin had more interest in other directions. The absence of a sound frontier policy only indicates that 'Alauddin could not rise above the mediocre standard of Medieval Rajput monarchs of India. That towards the later part of his reign no Mongol invasions occurred was because of the altered situation in Transoxiana and not because of his effective measures.

3

The Deccan Policy of Alauddin Khalji

Eminent scholars have made asservations that 'Alaud-din Khalji's invasions of the Deccan and South were in nature mere plundering raids, and were similar to the raids of Mahmud of Ghaxna on Northern India.[1] However, on examination of the sources I am led to draw different conclusions. The present paper, therefore aims at placing the findings before the scholarly world for their perusal.

The first raid of 'Alaud-din took place during the reign of his uncle Jalalud-din Firuz Khalji and at a time when he was Governor of Kara. So far as the motive of this expedition is concerned it is difficulty to say anything with absolute certainty, but the result certainly proved to be of far-reaching consequences both for the North as well as for the South. According to Barani, 'Alauddin was so troubled by his wife and mother-in-law that he wanted to conquer some country where he might stay and never return home.[2] Nizamuddin[3] and Badaoni[4] have simply copied the statement of Barani. The statement of Barani, however, logically does not fit in with his own subsequent narrative, wherein he mentions that 'Alaud-din while going out for the expedition had taken all possible measures to keep in touch with his own iqta' and had left his interest in the hands of his trusted friend 'Alaul Kulk; and he had also kept a line of contract with the centre through his brother Ulugh Khan. If the motive of 'Aaud-

---

1. S. K. Aiyangar ; *South India and her Mohamamdan Invaders* pp,74-76 82-84, 86, 90-91, 123.
   N. Venkataramanayya, *The Early Muslim Expansion in South India*, pp. 14-71.
   K. S. Lal, *History of the Khaljis*, pp. 219-20.
2. Barani, *Farikh-i-Firuzshahi* p. 221 (Henceforth referred as *Barani*).
3. *Tabaqat-i-Akbari*, p. 129.
4. Badaoni, *Muntakhib-ut-Tawarikh*, I, (Tr. Ranking), p. 237.

din was to leave the kingdom of Delhi for good, where was the need of such measures.

'Isami[5] says that 'Alaud-din wanted to invade Deogiri to collect wealth from there. From the version of Isami it seems that 'Alaud-din's ambition had been flared up by his knowlede of the growing unpopularrity of Jalalud-din Khalji among the Khalji Turks. Alaud-din's expedition to Bhilsa undertaken with the permission of the Sultan,[6] had not only enhanced his prestige and improved his resources—as he was granted to retain the entire revenues of Kara and Awadh by the doting Sultan[7]—but had furnished him with he stil more valuable infomation about the fabulous wealth of Deogiri. Under the circumstance 'Alaud-din must have considered the wealth of Deogiri as the most essential[8] aid for acquiring the throne of Delhi and therefore worth its wager. The motive of 'Alaud-din therefore was primarily to conduct a plundering raid into Deogiri, and the success achieved by him was certainly beyond his expectation.[9]

Ramchandra, the ruler of Deogiri agreed to send yearly the revnue of Illichpur and its dependncies to 'Alaud-din at Kara by way of annual tribute. Ram Chandra also gave in marriage one of his daughters to Alaud-din.[10] In return Alauddin handed over to Ram Chandra his royal umbrella

---

5. 'Isami, *Futuh-us-Salatin*, (Agra Text), p. 221. Henceforth referred as '*Isami*'.
6. *Barani*, p. 220.
7. *Barani* p. 220.
8. *Barani*, p. 220, Barani here says that when 'Alaud-din received information of the wealth and elephants of Deogiri he decided that after reaching kara he would collect a large army and invade Deogiri without informing Sultan Jalalud-din Khalji.
9. *Firishta*, I, p. 167. All references of Firishta are from the Bombay Text.
10. '*Isami*, p. 228.

(*chatra*), two elephantss as well as his entire territory.[11] In short 'Alauddin reinstated Ram Chandra at Deogiri and made it a permanent source of income for himself. That 'Alauddin concluded the treaty on his own behalf is clear from the terms of the treaty whereby the tribute was to be sent to him at Kara and not to Delhi which was the apital and the seat of the Sultan.

No doubt, the Deccan gold proved instrumental in fulfilling the ambition of 'Aladddin, i.e. occupation of the throne of Delhi, but that was not all. The anuual tribute from Deogiri must have been a great aid to 'Alauddin inwading through the difficulties of the earlier years of his accession. That, even in his affluence, 'Alauddin was not altogether oblivious of the Deccan, can be easily deduced from the expedition that he sent to Warangal[12] under Malik Juna Dad Bak and Malik Jhaju, the muqti of Kara. This expedition which was sent through Bengal and had ended in a miserable failure, must have convinced 'Alauddin of the futility of of attempts on the Southern kingdoms from that quarter.

The arrangement made 'Alauddin' at Deogiri worked smoathly only for some time, as we learn from Barani that Ramchandra who had been regularly sending the annual tribute to 'Alauddin' at Delhi, for some time prior to A.D. 1308, discontinued the tribute.[13] It is quite likely that the long absence of Muslim arms from the Deccan, the distance of Deogiri from Delhi, the preoccupation of Alauddin with the Rajputs and the news of the disgrace of Delhi army in Telingana, might have been some of the factors that had led Ramdeo to take such a course of action. 'Islami,[14] however, says that it was Bhillama, the son of Ramchandra, who had revolted against the authority of Delhi and had imprisoned

11. *'Isami*, p. 230 verses 4480-83.
12. *Barani*, p. 300 ; *Badaoni*, I, (Ranking) p. 265 ; *Firishta*, I, p. 195.
13. *Barani*, p. 326 ; *Khazain-ul-Futuh*, (Tr), p. 51.
14. *'Isami*, p. 274.

Ramchandra ; that it was Ramchandra who had actually informed 'Alaud-din about the changed situation in Deogiri and had requested the Sultan to send an able person with an army to put down the rebellion and restore his authority. The two different versions however agree on the issue that 'Alaud-din's motive in sending Malik Kafur to the Deccan in 1308 was to re-establish his authority over Deogiri.

As for the result of Malik Kafur's invasion of Deogiri the following points may be noted. Ramchandra was defeated and along with his family he was imprisoned.[15] Malik Kafur took possession of the country in the name of his master and distributed it among his officers.[16] Malik Kafur brought Ramchandra along with his relations to Delhi where 'Alaud-din treated him well and after a stay of six months permitted him to return bestowing on him many hours as well as the title of *Rai Rayan*.[17] Alauddin not only restored his kingdom but added to it the district of Navasari.[18] Besides. Ramchandra was given a canopy (*chatra*) and some cash[19] to defray the travelling expenses of the return journey.

From the facts enumerated above it is clear that 'Alaud-din was pursuing a calculated policy of reducing the Yadava territory of Deogiri into a subordinate or a feudatory state, whose ruler would be his dependent and look after hii interest. 'Alauddin could not have adopted a better yolicy than this. Such a policy established his suzerainty and ensured him a regular revenue without adding burden io the exchequer. The removal of Ramchandra and the appointment of a governor and officers from Delhi would have only added more responsibility and increased his problems without adding anything

15. *Khazain-ul-Futuh*, (Tr.) p. 52.
16. *Firishta*, I, p. 206.
17. *Barani*, p. 326 ; *Isami* p. 276 ; *Firishta* I, p. 206 ; *Khazain-ul-Futuh* (Tr.), p. 53.
18. *Firishta*, I. p. 206.
19. Two lacs according to 'Isami and one lac according to Firishta.

to the efficiency of the administrative machinery. Justification of 'Ala-ud-din's policy can be found from the subsequent behaviour of Ramchandra. During the remaining years of his life Ramchandra not only stood firm in his loyalty to the Sultan[20] but also rendered valuable service to the Imperial army that was sent to subdue the Hindu kingdoms of the South. Next year (1309 A.D.) when Malik Kafur was sent to reduce Telingana, Ramchandra welcomed him and made arrangements for the comfort of Delhi army. He also issued instructions that grain dealers and others should arrange for the sale of commodities at a fair price and also look after their needs.[21]

Ramchandra also supplied a contingent of Maratha soldiers as reinforcement to the army of Delhi.[22] Thus we find that for all practical purposes Ramchandra was loyally performing all the duties that any governor of the place would have done. That Deogiri was considered as a part of the empire can also be deduced from the fact that Malik Kafur from the time he had entered the territory (jurisdiction) of Deogiri, had seen that no damage was done to the people nor were they plundered by the soldiers.[23]

After succcssfully establishing his authority over Deogiri, 'Alaud-din turned towards Warangal which was the capital of the kingdom of Telingana. According to Amir Khusrau, by the orders of the Sultan, Malik Kafur started on another expedition, this time to reduce the country of Telingana on 25th Jamadi I 709 A. H.[24] 31st October, 1309 A. D. The motive and policy of 'Ala-ud-din can be easily discerned from the advice that he gave to Malik Kafur on the eve of his departure for Telingana. After giving some advcie on care and caution, 'Ala-ud-din advised Malik Kafur to cap-

20. All contemporary historians agree on this point.
21. *Barani*, p. 328 ; *Firishta*, I, P. 208.
22. *ibid*.
23. *Khazain-ul-Futuh*, (Tr.) p. 58.
24. *ibid*, p 56.

ture the fort of Warangal and overthrow Pratap Rudra Deo (Laddar Deo) ; and if Pratap Rudra Deo agreed to surrender all his treasure and elephants and also agreed to pay annual tribute thereafter, he was not to insist on more. He should not also insists on the Raja to present himself in person at Dehli.[25]

Thus we find that one of the aims of 'Ala-ud-din was to reduce Warangal to the samp status of a subordinate territory as had been accorded to the kingdom of Deogiri.

It was on 13th Ramzan 709 A.H./March 1310 A. D. that Malik Kafur succeeded in capturing the outer fort of Warangal[26] and besiged Pratap Rudra Deo who had taken shelter in the inner fort. When the siege of the inner fort was prolonged, Pratap Rudra Deo lost his courage and opened negotiations for peace and finally surrendered himself.[27]

By the treaty that was concluded Pratap Rudra Deo handed over the accumulated wealth in the fort of Warangal and consented to the payment of annual tribute.[28] Malik Kafur also sent a *chatra* (conopy) and *Khilat*[29] (robe of honour) on behalf of the Sultan recognising thereby the submission of Pratap Rudra Deo.

The payment of annual tribute and acceptance of *chatara Khilat* are certainly marks of acknowlegment of the overlordship of 'Ala-ud-din Khalji. Pratap Rudra Deo carried out his obligations faithfully even after the return of Malik Kafur.[30]

---

25. *Barani*, p, 327 ; *Firishta*, I, p. 208.
26. *Khazain-ul-Futuh*, (Tr.), p. 68.
27. *ibid*, p. 78.
28. *Barani*, p. 330 ; *Firishta*, I, p. 208 ; *Khazaininul Futuh*, (Tr.). p. 78, Amir Khusru also speaks of the fixation of the *Khiraj* and *jiziya* for Laddar Deo.
29. *'Isami*, p. 283.
30. The arrival of the tribute from Pratap Rudra Deo is mentioned by Barani (vide, *Barani*, p. 334).

According to Amir Khusrau, within a few weeks of his return to the capital, Malik Kafur was summoned by the Sultan and was asked to lead an expedition to Mabar and proclaim the Muslim faith in that far off region [31] The phrase 'the light of *shariat* may reach', in fact, is the form of Amir Khusrau to indicate the Sultan's desire to establish his suzerainty there. If Sultan 'Ala-ud-din had been particular about spreading the Muslim faith, he certainly would had done so in Deogiri and Warangal. Besides Malik Kafur was also asked to subjugate Ballal Deo the ruler of Dwarsamudra.[32]

When Vir Ballal III, the Hoysala rular of Dwarsamudra, heard about the arrival of Malik Kafur before the citadel on 5th Shawal 710/Feb 25, 1311 A. D.,[33] he held counsel and sought the advice of his commanders and ministers. It is not that Vir Ballal was caught unawares. No doubt he had gone out towards the kingdom of the Pandayas of Mabar, but had returned to his capital on receiving the news of Malik Kafur's entry into his kingdom. He had also sought and received reinforcement from Vir Pandya. But Vir Ballal, who knew that rulers like Ramchandra and Pratap Rudra Deo had submitted earlier, was not willing to offer a futile resistance[34] and thereby expose the people to hardship. Vir Ballal opened negotiations and sent Balak Deva Naik as his agents[35] According to Amir Khusrau Malik Kafur conveyed that the orders of the Caliph concerding Ballal Deo and all other *Rais* are :

31. *Khazain-ul-Futuh*, p. 80. According to Amir Khusrau, Malik Kafur, started on 26th Jamadi II, 710.
32. *Barani*, p. 333 ; *Isami*, p 285.
33. *Khazain-ul-Futuh* (Tr.), p. 87.
34. *ibid*, p. 89.
35. The terms offered by Vir Ballal may be quoted here in the words of Amir Khusrau :—
"This servant Balal Deo submits to the Emperor, like Laddar Deo and Ram Deo, and whatever the Solomon of the time commands, I am ready to obey. If you

(*Continued on next page*)

First, I am to place before them the two negatives of the oath of affirmation and if they fail to see the light, I am to offer them the alternative of having the yoke of tribute (*Zimma*) put on their necks. If they reject this also and refuse to pay tribute, then I will not place any burden on necks but will simply relieve their necks of the burden of their heads.[36]

Vir Ballal agreed to pay annual tribute and came in person to make his submission before Malik Kafur.

After setting the affairs of Dwarsamudra, Malik Kafur marched into the territory of the Pandyas of Mabar guided by Vir Ballal III[37]. Malik Kafur had started from Dwarsamudra on 18th *Siawal* 710/ March 10, 1311 A.D., and moved from place to place collecting wealth and pursuing Vir Pandya, who was all the time succesfully eluding him, till 4th *Zilhijjah* 710/April 25, 1311 A. D.,[38] when Malik Kafur finally declared that he was returning to Dehli. Malik Kafur had relentlessly searched the Rai for weeks and months ; in towns, in jungles and in hills but every where in vain.[39] If Malik Kafur's aim was mere plunder why this searching for the Rai, because so far as wealth was concerned it could be and was plundered even in the absence of the Rai. It therefore, clearly indicates, that besides plunder, the real aim of Malik Kafur was something else i.e. submission of the Rai in person. It may be pointed out in passing that Vir Balal III accompanied Malik Kafur

---

(*Continued from previous page*)

desire horses like demons, elephants like gaints and other valuables, they are present. If all this noise and tumult is for the destruction of the four walls of this fort, they are, as they stand no obstacle to your advance. The fort is the fort of the Sultan, take it. And what can be better for me than to keep my stones to myself, and remain out of harms 'sway like the Hindus of Deogiri".

36. *Khazain-ul-Futuh*, (Tr.) p. 91.
37. *Isami*, p. 287.
38. *Khazain-ul-Futuh*, (Tr.), p. 107.
39. Lal, *History of the Khalijis*, p. 212.

to Delhi, where Sultan 'Alaud-din was pleased with him, because of his help and loyalty, and gave him a special robe of honour, a crown and a *chatra* and also a purse of ten lecs of tanakas. The Sultan also restored him to the territory of Dwarsamudra.[40]

From the events narrated, it will be clear that 'Alaud-din was following a calculated policy of reducing the kingdoms of the Deccan and the South as tributary states which would accept his suzerainty, pay annual tribute and act in all manners as his subordinates. 'Ala-ud-din certainly was conscious that administration of these places from distant Dehli was a very difficult task, because if the rulers of these kingdoms were removed, it might lead to local resistance and would create trouble of which he had already enough in the North. It certainly was an imperialistic policy and it can be said that by establishing his own officers he could have hardly achieved more than what he actually achieved by his policy. That Ala-ud-din had established his authority and suzerainty in the Deccan and the South is also borne out by one of the Jain works, *Nabinandana-jinodhara-prabandha*[41] which was composed in V. S. 1393/1336 A. D.

Two verses of this work clearly illustrate the point :—

(i) "Going to Devagiri he captured its ruler, but reinstated him there to serve as it were a pillar of his victory (III).

(ii) "Resembling Indra in prowess, he (Ala-ud-din Khalji) brought under his control the rulers of Karnata, Pandu and Tilanga countries (III' 7).

'Ala-ud-din's policy of extending his empire beyond the Vindhyas is further illustrated by the measures he took after the death of Ramchandra, the ruler of Deogiri. Alaud-din had adopted the policy of allowing the Hindu rulers to continue in their territories after they had accepted his suzarainty.

40. *'Isami*, p. 290.
41. *Indian Historical Quarterly*. Vol. XXXII, 1956, p. 96.

But Singhana, the successor of Ramchandra, severed his connection with Dehli and began to rule independently. Alaud-din, therefore, had to send Malik Kafur, who was already well acquainted with the affairs of the Deccan to re-establish his authority. Since Singnana was persistent in his hostility towards Dehli, Alaud-din appointed Malik Kafur as governor of Deogiri and commissioned him with the task of crushing all hostility.[42] Malik Kafur occupied Deogiri and by his military activity inspired such terror into the hearts of neighbouring terri tories that the last remnants of opposition to the Dehli govern ment were wiped out.[43] Thus we may point out that if plunder was the only aim it could again have been achieved simply by marching through the territories and collecting spoils.

We can therefore, say with greater certainty that one of the aims of 'Ala-ud-din's Deccan policy was territorial expansion ; as far as wealth is concerned, it always accompanies territorial expansion, in the shape of added revenue. In the case of 'Ala-ud-din it was more because it meant annual tribute without incurring any administrative expenditure.

42. *Isami,* p. 326.
43. Lal, *History of the Khaljis,* p. 216.

4

Market Regulation of Alauddin Khilji

Many aspects of Medieval Indian History have become highly controvertial, but perhaps none more than the economic reforms of Ala-ud-din Khalji. While a group[1] of historians have discovered him as the greatest monarch of medieval India, Dr. P. Saran could find in him no good, except the happy trait in his character of ' respecting the advice of his councillors and ministers and adopting their proposals wherever he found himself in difficulty[2]. To the learned scholar Ala-ud-din Khalji stands condemned for his selfish motives and his desire for personal gain and being obsessed by this discovery he had laboriously worked out the miseries that the control of prices entailed on the people of all walks of life[3]. Starngely enough, the scholars of these two different views have only tried to examine the personality of the Khalji monarch and have projected his economic reforms in that light. While all of them agree that Barani is confused in his narrative, none-the-less and unhesitatingly, they have accepted much of the causal sequence maintained by him, and have accepted such portions of narratives as fitted in best in their own pattern of logic. The present paper, however, without entering into their controversies, aims at examining the genesis of the market regulations and for the source of information it too depends primarily on Barani.

Without distracting merit of the work Zia-ud-din Barani we have to bear in mind the time and conditions under which he wrote his *Taarikh-i-Firozshahi* (1357 A.D.). He not only wrote after fifty years of actual occurrence but also under adverse circumstances and that too most probably without

---

1. Qureshi, *Administration of the Sultanate of Delhi* ; Ishwari Prasad, *History of Muslim Rule in India*, pp. 98-99 ; *Islamic Culture*, 1944, p. 45.
2. P. Saran, *Studies in Medieval Indian History*, p. 151.
3. *ibid*, (Economic Policy of Ala-ud-din Khalji). p. 182.

notes or reference works.[4] Under these circumstances with a mental make up for causal sequence Barani relates events in order of cause and effect as they had got fixed in his mind. His narratives, therefore, often create problems in reconstruction. In the absence of any other source material, however, his habit of repetitions often comes to our rescue, because he is not consistent in the details of his repetitions and mentions things which he had left or forgotten elsewhere earlier.

One such cause and effect fixation in the mind of Barani we find in his treatment of the market regulations of Ala-ud-din Khalji. Accorning to Bararni, Ala-ud-din wanted to pay the small sum of 234 tankas to his cavalry soldier with one horse and on his asking for advice if this would work, his counsellors pointed out that this could be possible only if the Sultan could reduce the prices of the commodities of daily use,[5] or in other words, if the Sultan could increase the purchasing power of the solidiers by lowering the prices. Thus to Barani the cause of fixation of the prices and establishment of control over the market was the Sultan's desire to pay to the soldiers a salary which to his mind was a small amount. It seems that Barani saw the fact of an increased army and the fact of low and stable prices and converted a simple co-relation into a simple causation. In his narrative, however, Barani does not mention the extent of reduction of the salary and the amount that the soldiers received prior to the introduction of this salary. He also does not mention the names of the members of the advisory council or even the name of a single member who advised him on these lines. This silence of Barani leads to two questions, one, was the salary reduced or it was simply an introduction of cash salary in place of revenue assignment (iqta), and two, was there actual reduction in the price of the commodities or simply fixing a ceiling on the prices to prevent them from rising higher than the prices prevalent in Delhi.

4. Habib, *Political Theory of the Delhi Sultanate*, pp. 121-122.
5. Barani, *Tarikh-i-Firuzshahi*, p 304.

Regarding the first question we are led to conclude that cash salary was introduced for the first time since Turkish conquest, for the simple reason that cash salary is not mentioned prior to Ala-ud-din Khalji, on the contrary we are informed by the chroniclers that land assignment or *iqtas* were granted to the soldiers in lieu of their salary. The change over to cash payment to the soldiers was bound to result in an increase in the cash in circulation. As for the amount of salary we find that Ala-ud-din gave 234 tankas[6] per year i.e., 19½ tankas per month. This amount certainly was not a small sum for the first decade of the fourteenth century when we find that Akbar calculated the salary of a *tabinan* at the rate of Rs. 240/- per annum while during the reign of Shah Jahan it was Rs. 200/- per annum. Thus Ala-ud-din paid to a soldier only Rs. 6/- per annum less that what Akbar paid and Rs. 34/- per anaum more than what Shah Jahan paid. We cannot, therefore, say that Ala-ud-din paid a low salary to his soldiers.

However, the basis on which Ala-ud-din fixed the salary of a soldier at this rate is a question which remains unsolved, and with the information available to us for the present, at best, a suggestion can be made. Just as Ala-ud-din had fixed the produce of *Biswa* as unit of measurement on the basis of some data not known to us, he might have similarly arrived at this figure on the basis of some calculations which have not yet been discovered.

Before taking up the nature of the fixation of prices it would be better to ascertain the region or the area over which the price control was to be effective. Barani mentions of the stability of price in the *Mandi*, the effectiveness of the *Shahna-i-mandi* and also says that prices remained stable even under adverse conditions i.e. even the failure of rains did not affect the price of grain in the *Mandi*, because the state store-houses contained enough grain to be released to the market in case

6. The tanka of Ala-ud-din was of Silver and weighed 96 ratis.

of shortage of supply in the *Mandi*. This *mandi* as referred by Barani was situated in Delhi. Thus we find that the prices of the commodities as fixed by Ala-ud-Din were meant for Delhi alone. The next important question that arises out of this is, why was the fixation of prices for the market of Delhi alone ? If the contention that prices were fixed at cheap rates to enable the soldiers to meet their expenses out of the salary that was paid to them, is accepted, the obvious deduction should be that the entire army recruited was to remain in Delhi where the controlled prices operated. But we know for certain that the army was posted at Dipalpur, Samana, Sunam and other provincial cities, Thus we find that there is flaw in the causal sequence given by Barani. Being unable to comprehend other factors Barans has simply weaved in a causal sequence to explain the phenomenon.

So far the actual control of prices was concerned, we find Ala-ud-din issuing a very comprehensive list which included all possible articles of consumption, such as foodgrains, bread, vegetables, cloth and all kinds of piece goods, male and female slaves, milch cattle, beasts of burden, horses and various articles of merchandise. A close examination of the steps taken by Ala-ud-din to ensure the effectiveness of the control of prices regarding these commodities will roveal the genesis and the nature of market control regulations. Such a comprehensive control required strict vigilance and for this purpose Ala-ud-din set up a new department to look after the affairs of the market. Overall charge of the market was given to Malik Qabul Ulugh Khani with the title of *Shahna-i-Mandi* and for his prestige and dignity he was granted a large *iqta* with a contigent of horses and a large number of foot-soldiers which included peons, bailifs etc. He was also provided with a number of *naib-shahnas* (assistants) to assist him in looking after the various branches of the market. To create team effect these *naibs* were picked up from the trusted friends of Malik Qabul.

We can start our examination with the control of grain because it was considered that the pricer of all other commodities of human need were governed by the prices of grain[7]. Regarding the prices of grain as fixed by the Sultan, Barani supplies us with the following list :[8]

Wheat :	7½ Jitals, per man
Barley :	4 ,, ,, ,,
Paddy :	5 ,, ,, ,,
Pulse (Urad) :	5 ,, ,, ,,
Gram :	5 ,, ,, ,,
Moth :	3 ,, ,, ,,

Ala-ud-din seems to have fully recognised that the stability of prices depended on adequate supply and to ensure it he took a number of measures. He ordered that the land revenue from the *Khalsa* land and the region of *doab* shonld be collected in grain[9] and sent to Delhi through caravans (*banjaras*) where it was stocked in government store houses. Barani says that by this method so much grain reached Delhi that there was scarcely a street which did not contain two or three royal store-houses filled with grain and when there was scarcity of rain or the caravans for some cause or other failed to convey sufficient grain into the market it was released to the market from the royal stores to be sold at government fixed rates and supplied to the people according to their wants[10].

Since the working of the system was dependent upon the co-operation of the traders (grain dealers) who were to transport the grain in Delhi, it was exposed to serious weakness. Unless some sort of check was imposed upon them, they would not hesitate to make profit by fowl means i.e. by deliberate delay in conveying grain and thus causing scarcity in normal times or by sending grain out of Delhi and causing thereby artificial scarcity in the market and then make profit by black-market.

7. *Barani.* p. 304.
8. *ibid.*, p. 305.
9. *ibid.*, p. 306.
10. *ibid.*, p. 306.

To avoid such a possibility Ala-ud-din thought of keeping a rigorous vigilance and control over the merchants. For this purpose the grain dealers from all parts of the kingdom were consigned to the charge of Malik Qabul, *Shahna-i-Mandi*, to be governed and managed as if "they were the subject of the *Shahna-i-Mandi*". The *Shahna-i-Mandi* was instructed to keep the leaders (Muqqaddams) of the grain-dealers under fetters till they signed a deed of mutual security and brought their family and children and property and settled them in the villages bordering on the Jamna and pledged them as security for their honesty.[11] As will be evident, such measures were necessary to establish full control over them and not to coerce them to undergo loss as Dr P. Saran would have us believe. Of course, the loss that they had to suffer was the undue profits made through underhand dealings which in the changed conditions they were unable to make.

To be on the safe side for a constant supply to the market from the store-houses, Ala-ud-din wanted to build up a buffer stock and for this purpose he ordered the *Mutsarifs* and the *karkuns* to assist the licenced or authorised *banjaras* in purchasing grain from the cultivators. Ala-ud-din ordered that at the office of the *Wizarat* written engagements should be taken from the *Mutsarifs* and revenue cellectors of the country lying within *doab* to the effect that they would cause the grain to be delivered to the *banjaras* (caravans) by the cultivators at their own fields, and also that they would prevent the cultivators to carry off any large quantities of grain from the fields to their own houses and hoard it there. The obvious idea of the Sultan was to prevent the cultivators from hoarding and thus create scarcity and later sell it at a higher price. Barani at this stage clearly uses the word *ihtikar* and says that the purpose was prohibition against the hoarding up of grain and selling it at enhanced price[12]. Here if we consider, to what extent the ordinary cultivator was in

11. *ibid.*, p. 306.
12. *ibid.*, p. 304.

a position to Hoard, we will find that the ultimate hoarder in the rural area was the village *Baniya* who had hardly any scruples for making money.

These were the measures taken by Ala-ud-Din to maintain a constant supply to the market with a view to keep the price structure stable. The next question comes, whether the prices fixed by Ala-ud-din Khalji were lower than the prices prevalent in the country side and also that, were these lower than the normal [13] prices ? The view that the prices fixed by Ala-ud-din were lower than the prices prevalent in the country side becomes questionable for the reason that in such a case who bore the loss. Of course the state could subsidise but such a thing is difficult to be attributed to Ala-ud-din. If the cultivators or the *banjaras* had to bear the loss, it is difficult to accept that they could have stood it for the remaining years of the reign of Ala-ud-din Khalji which would come to about a decade. Thus the only possibility left is that the prices fixed by Ala-ud-din were not lower than the prices prevalent in the country side. Such a view is further corroborated by the statement of Barani, who says that the villagers for their personal benefit, used to bring personally as much of the grain as they could from their storage and used to sell them in the *mandi* at the government rates.[14] This statement certainly indicates that there was a margin of profit left to them in the prices fixed by the Sultan. Regardtng the question of normal prices, we find that the prices of the commodities as they prevailed during the reign of Firuz Shah Tughlak are not very different from the prices fixed by Ala-ud-din Khalji. The prices per maund of wheat, barley and paddy during the reign of Firuz Shah Tughlak were 8, 4 and 4 jitals respectively, whereas in Ala-ud-din's time they were 7½, 4 and 5 *jitals* respectively, *i.e.* if the price of wheat was half *Jital* less the price of paddy was 1 *jital* more. The author of *Tarikh-i-*

13. The word normal has not been used here as a terminology of Economics.

14. *ibid.*, pp. 307-8

Daudi[15] tells us that prices in Ibrahim Lodi's reign were cheaper than those in any other reign except Ala-ud-Din's. But Ala-ud-din had to use coercion whereas it was a natural phenomenon of Ibrahim's reign. It was, however, not a gift of Heaven as the contemporary chronicler would have us believe. It was an outcome of the Afghan system of granting *jagirs* that reduced the demand of food-grains in Delhi, besides the empire was much shrunk in size and was surrounded by independent kingdoms, which considerably reduced the importance of Delhi. It no longer remained the mart or the emporium of India and was relieved of the burden of the floating population. In others the demand in the time of Ibrahim Lodi was considerably reduced and the pressure on the supply was gone.

Thus we find that neither the prices fixed were lower then those in country-side nor were they below the normal prices but then the question arises: what was the need of fixing the prices and taking strong measures to see that these were obsrved. The real cause for all this lay in a slightly altered economic condition of Delhi during the reign of Ala-ud-din Khalji. Delhi in Ala-ud-din Khalji's time became the capital of a mighty empire and a central mart with a rapidly increasing population to which the constant movement of the merchants added a floating population. It also became a large cantonment. All this not merely intensified the demand for food-grains but also introduced a strong cash nexus and increased the money circulation. These factors inevitably produced inflationary conditions because the price of a commodity is not merely governed by the intensity of demand but also directly in proportion to the amount of money in circulation. This condition offered an opportunity to the business community to increase the prices by creating artificial scarcity Barani's statement clearly indicates that there was constant attempt at monopoly prices being charged by the merchants.

The condition of the market after the promulgation of regulations indicates the extent of restraint that Ala-ud-dir

15. *Tarikh-i-Daudi*, p. 104.

brought about over the activities of the merchant community. According to Barani, "the *Shahna-i-Mandi* had to furnish a list of prices and report on the condition of the bazar. The *Barid-Mandi* reported on the quality of the articles. The informers who had been appointed for every bazar made their reports to the Sultan. If there were discrepancies between the reports of the informers and that of the *Barid* and of the *Shahna*, the *Shahna* was punished. But as the officers appointed in the bazars knew that the Sultan got his reports on the transactions and the state of market from these sources, it was impossible to deviate even in the least, from the bazar regulations." Even under adverse conditions neither the grain of the Sultan nor the grain of the merchants could indeed rise a single *dang* above the rates fixed by the Sultan." In the seasons of drought the merchants of each quarter of the town received daily a supply of grain according to the number of inhabitants in each quarter and they issued grain to the common people not exceeding a *mann* per individual at the government fixed prices. Rich people and the notables also, who were not in possession of villages and lands, got grain from the market. If during the season of drought poor and helpless people crowded the bazars and got crushed to death and the officers neglected to pay attention to the influx, the matter was immediately reported to the Sultan and the *Shahna* had to suffer for it."[16]

Thus we find that Ala-ud-din's motive was to check the rising prices which was due to manipulation of the business community and not to reduce the prices to a lower level than the normal. This will be still more clear from an examination of the regulations relating to control on supply and the prices fixed for other commodities.

The first regulation mentioned by *Barani* for the control of prices and sale of cloth is the establishment of a special market named *Sarai-Adl*. For the establishment of *Sarai-Ald* the open

16. *Tarikh-i-Firuzshahi*, Text, p. 309 ; (Tr.) J. A. S. B. 1870, p. 28.

space inside the Badayun gate in the direction of *Kaushak-i-Sabz* which for years had not been used, was selected, and the Sultan gave orders that no cloth either purchased with the money advanced by the State or those brought by the merchants of the town and its neighbouring regions should be stored up in any place outside the *Sarai-Adl* and that the cloth was to be sold at the price fixed by the Sultan inside the Sarai. He also ordered that if anyone violated this rule his stock of cloth was to be confiscated by the government.[17] Besides cloth, sugar, ghee, edible oils and salt was also to be sold in the *Sarai-Adl*.

The setting up of a special market as mentioned by Barani, was certainly a necessity if the control of the price was to be effective. No government, certainly not the government of Ala-ud-din of medieval times, could effectively establish a control over the market if it remained scattered all over the city. For the facility of the purchasers, Ala-ud-din ordered the market of *Sarai-Adl* to remain open from early morning till the time of the last prayer. Regarding the efficiency and usefulness of the market, Barani says that people thus got what they needed and no one returned disappointed.[18]

The setting up of a specified market also indicates that Ala-ud-din wanted to keep a regular check over the merchants who used to come to the capital from different parts of the kingdom. Unless these merchants were kept under proper control they would, by their superior purchasing power, upset the price structure which the Sultan wanted to maintain. It was with this aim that he took two definite steps : first, he ordered the *Shahna* of the market to maintain a register of the names of merchants, both Hindus and Muslims, belonging to the city of Delhi as well as to the neighbouring regions, and also to take an undertaking from them that they would sell at government rates all the commodities that they bring to

17. *Barani* p. 309.
18. *ibid.*, p. 310.

the market.[19] Thus while no restriction was imposed on them to bring their commodity, rather they were encouraged, they were prevented from raising the price in the market. Secondly, he placed the cloth market of *Sarai-Adl* in the charge of rich Multani merchants to whom advance up to the extent of twenty lacs of *tankas* was made to facilitate them for purchasing cloth from different parts where they were produced and to bring them for sale in the *Sarai-Adl*. By the second method he not only succeeded in procuring the products of different places at their local rates but also succeed in maintaining a constant flow of the supply. Barani says that whenever the cloth of other merchants for some reason or other could not reach, the cloth procured by this method met the demand of the market and thus kept the price level constant.[20]

Regarding costly varieties Barani says that Sultan Ala-uddin ordered that no one was to be allowed to purchase in *Sarai-Adl* the costly stuff, which were not used by the common man without a written permit from the *Shahna* of the market who was to issue such a permit only on receiving a written application from the purchaser stating therein his requirements and purpose. Barani also says that the *Shahna* used to give permits to the *Amirs* and *Maliks* and other great and respectable persons only after being satisfied of their genuine requirements.[21]

The system of procuring the products of different parts of the country at once made Delhi an emporium where they were readily available. The supply of the costly varieties was limited ; and as they were produced in far and distant places widely separated from each other and yet available in Delhi, there was every chance for the merchants from different parts to be tempted to purchase them at Delhi for carrying them to their respective areas, where they were rare, on their return

19. *ibid.*, pp. 310-311.
20. *ibid.*, pp. 310-311.
21. *ibid.*, p. 311.

homeward journey. Therefore, unless some restriction and check was imposed the shortage of supply would result in no time. The merchants would also not hesitate to pay a higher price for such species to individuals who could purchase them from *Sarai-Adl*. It was to prevent such operations that Ala-ud-din adopted the strict measure of permit-system. Barani also says that the reason for the introduction of the pass system was to prevent merchants, both of the city and the outsiders, from obtaining costly stuffs from the *Sarai-Adl* at the rates fixed by the Sultan, and then taking them to other places where they could not be had and selling them at high prices.[22]

The difference in the prices as mentioned by Barani, does not refer to the difference in prices fixed by the Sultan and the prices prevalent in the areas of their production.[23] It refers to the prices of those areas where such varieties were not easily available. Since the Multani merchants purchased these commodities from the areas where they were actually produced they had not to pay more than the rates fixed by the Sultan for Delhi and, therefore, they had not to bear any loss.[24] Of course, they were prevented from making huge profits by their nefarious underhand dealings in Delhi ; and if we consider it a loss they certainly had to undergo it.

The regulations mentioned by Barani, in connection with the sale and the prices of live stock, evince the same care on the part of the Sultan to stop profiteering or black-marketing. Barani mentions that after fixing the prices of the horses according to their class and quality, the Sultan prohibited the dealers and moneyed men from purchasing animals in the

22. *ibid.*, p. 312.
23. For the view of Dr. P. Saran see : *Studies in Medieval Indian Hiitory*, p. 170.
24. P. Saran, *Loc cit.*, p. 173, Dr Saran says "It is therefore clear that the Multani and other marchants were made to suffer this loss themselves."

market or employing anyone to purchase on their behalf.[25] The dealers and the moneyed men as referred by Barani were certainly not the consumers. They were interested in regrating and making excess profit by demanding fancy princes from those who were in need of the beast. Barani himself says that they for years had been getting a profit and gaining livelihood by traffic in horses and were in leauge with the chief brokers of the market.[26] This statement clearly indicates an underhand dealing on the part of such intermediaries. To check their activity Ala-ud-din prohibited such dealers from approaching the horse-market. Some of them were fined and some with the cheif brokers were banished to distant fortresses. It seems in spite of such an order some chief horse-brokers persisted in their activity for Barani says that coercion and castigation had to be applied to the important horse brokers, who were most arrogant, rebellious and audacious class of people in disobeying orders. The activity of this group in artificially raising the prices can best be given in the words of Barani who says that "these chief brokers are in reality the rulers of the market and until they are brought into order by coercion and castigation and cease taking bribes which they receive from both parties and abstain from mediating between the buyer and the seller, the price of horse can never fall.[27]

From the above citation it will be clear that a group of petty brokers who were in league with rich brokers used to manipulate the prices and increase them through negotiations with both the seller and buyer and what the Sultan did was to check their activity *i.e.* he prevented them from increasing the prices beyond a certain fixed limit as settled by him. As Barani says that "but for the harsh temperament of the Sultan it was difficult to bring these shameless brokers on the right path.[28]

25. *Barani,* p. 313.
26. *ibid.*
27. *ibid.*
28. *ibid.*

Regarding other live-stock and slaves both male and female, Ala-ud-din took similar measures as he had taken for the horses and by preventing the activity of the brokers maintained the price level as fixed by him.

Regarding other items of general merchandise Barani says that Sultan Ala-ud-din made strenous efforts and used to be constantly employed in appraising every article, however, slight it might be, such as needless, combs, shoes, slippers, pitchers, cups, tumblers etc. and the prices of all these he used to determine according to the estimated cost of the articles *with a fair profit to the seller* and the schedules or prices thus determined in his presence used to be sent to the Diwan-i-Riyasat."[29] In the above passage we find Barani clearly mentions that the Sultan while fixing the prices did allow a margin of profit to the sellers or vendors of these articles. Thus if he allowed normal profit to the vendor, how can we deduce that he denied the normal profit to the producer.

Thus from the nature of the regulations as analysed above we find that the market of Delhi had become extremely unsettled and that the trading community from top to bottom was trying to manipulate prices and were charging high prices by creating artificial shortage of supply. Barani mentions that "people of the market are shameless, bold, cunning mean, liars and debauched. Because they themselves fix the prices of their goods, and are masters of these prices, kings always have been troubled by them and ministers have failed to devise laws to regulate transaction of this forward set of people."[30]

The increase of the population in the capital as well as the floating population with cash available to purchase the necessities prompted the dealers to increase the prices. Sultan Ala-ud-din must have noticed this tendency of rising prices and on examination or enquiry found out the underhand deal-

29. *ibid.*, p. 316.
30. *ibid.*

ing of the traders. His real aim, therefore, was to check the rising of the prices by fixing the prices which he realised could only be kept under control by strictly checking and controlling the dealers and also by inflicting exemplary punishments to those who violated his orders. His motive was to prevent the prices from rising beyod a certain level and not in lowering them and if there was any reduction it must have been in such cases where the traders had started demanding fancy prices.

Regarding the effect of these measures of Ala-ud-din we find even Barani saying that the regulations were of great benefit to the general people. The rich trading community might have found it to their disadvantage the regulations which deprived them of their excess profits, but to the common man the measures of Ala-ud-din must have meant a great blessing and a source of comfort. The statement of Hamid Qalandar that "people used to pay homage to his (Ala-ud-din Khalji's) tomb, put sacred thread on his grave, beg for boons and their wishes were fulfilled," truely speaking depicts the real feeling of the common people of Delhi for Ala-ud-din who could think of him in such a light.

5

Revenue Reforms of Alauddin Khalji

During the 13th century the Sultans of Delhi could hardly get any respite to organise and take adequate steps to introduce reforms in the direction of land revenue. The contemporary chroniclers are silent even regarding the state demand of the share of the produce, not to speak anything about the method of assessment. It may be partly because the Turkish occupation was mostly confined to the urban areas and the territories were assigned in *iqta* to various military commanders and officers of the state who collected their share from the local headmen commonly designated as *rais, muqaddam, chaudharis* and *khuts*. In granting *iqta* relation of service and area granted was hardly taken into consideration. Tht government had no means to ascertain the income of the *iqtadars*. The first step in this direction was taken by Balban who introduced the office of *khwajgi*. The *khwaja* was an officer appointed by the Central government and posted in the *iqta* ; his function being to record the income of the *iqta* and transfer the information to the Central government. Beyond this Balban could hardly achieve anything more. His views on revenue as found from his advice to his son--if we pay any credence to Barani's testimony--did not go beyond recommending that excessive demand should not be made even if there may be precedence ; that assessment should not be too high or else the peasantry would dessert the field, but it should not be at the same time so low as to leave a large surplus with the peasantry and encourage idleness and rebellion among them.[1]

The credit of taking definite steps to organise land revenue, goes to Sultan Ala-ud-din Khalji. Barani's account of Ala-ud-din's revenue arrangement attracted the attention of

1. Barani, *Tarikh-i-Firuzshahi*, Bib. Ind. Text, p. 100 (Hence forth simply Barani).

Moreland[2] as early as the twenties of the present century, who, following the lines of arguement of the chronicler deduced that the motives behind Ala-ud-din's policy were not really economic but his desire to built up a strong and centralised state. However, it may be pointed out that such a desire was not exceptional to Ala-ud-din. A medieval monarch could hardly conceive beyond it. The reasons adduced by Moreland for such a desire on the part of Al-ud-din, when summarised comes as follows : (1) Ala-ud-din came to the throne not through natural succession but through murder which led to a general resentment against him. This resentment, Ala-ud-din was afraid could be used against him by his enemies. (2) Across the frontiers Mongols were threatening the empire while within the empire local chiefs were in a rebellious mood, even in the court the nobles were conspiring against him. In order to meet these two dangers Ala-ud-din had to built up a powerful army which needed vast economic resources. The reasoning of Moreland presupposes that before Ala-ud-din all the rulers came by natural succession which we know was not the case ; and secondly that Mongol menace was new in the time of Ala-ud-din, which again we know had existed since Chingiz Khan came to the banks of the Indus. Besides, a comparison with Barani's account would indicate that Moreland has simply paraphrased Barani without critically examining his statements.

As already pointed out, the financial organisation prior to Ala-ud-din was based on the working of the *iqtadari* system where the pivotal role was played by middlemen. Besides, the rulers had been granting lands in *waqf* and *inam* to gain favour or support of a certain section of the Muslim community. These grantees, in the absence of efficient machinery to look after them, kept on increasing the areas of their holdings without government sanction. The grantees of the *waqfs* and *inams*, belonging to the class of *ulama* held that they

2. Moreland, *The Agrarian System of Moslem India*, (Allahabad) pp. 31, 32. (Henceforth simply Moreland).

enjoyed the grants not as favour of the monarch but in their own right as *ulama*. The revenue assigness (*iqtadars*) extracted as much as they could but entered lesser amounts in the revenue returns which they were required to send to the royal treasury. The outcome of such a situation was that the peasantry, which had to bear the burden, suffered from their exploitation, the grantees grew rich and powerful whereas the centre found itself always in need of resources. Such a situation could not have endured for ever and a reform by somebody had to be brought in sometime, and it came to the lot of Ala-ud-din to do so. May be, the rebellions highlighted the malady but the reforms were an outcome of historical process, Ala-ud-din being merely a tool in implimenting them.

Ala-ud-din Khalji directed his concern first of all towards the agencies which were collecting revenue from the cultivators. His aim was to put an effective check upon their increasing income. Of course he could not abolish the *iqtadari* system because there was no other alternative machinery to replace it. His greater concern seems to have been in establishing effective control on the holders of *milk*, *inam* and *waqf*. These grantees enjoyed the benifits but had not to render any service. To bring these grantees under effective control he revoked these grants.[3] Such a measure of Ala-ud-din should have caused wide spread resentment among the *ulama*, but we know nothing of the kind happened in his reign. The reason is not to be sought in the stern attitude of the Sultan and a strong standing army, but in the manner in which the Sultan implimented his policy. Ala-ud-din while resuming the grants did not deprive these grantees of their means of subsistance. Barani, in another place and in another context, mentions about the existance of such lands which had continued from the reign of Ala-ud-din Khalji.[4] What Ala-ud-din actually seems to have done was, first of all he resumed all grants and subsequently made fresh grants to individual

3. Barani, p. 284.
4. *ibid*., p. 439.

holders on their merit, and also granted them documents in which details of the grants were entered. His aim in taking such steps was, as pointed out by Dr. Tripathi, to assert the right of the monarch" to deel with all classes of lands, cancelled all such grants which he did not approve and bestowed others on his own terms."[5] One can easily discern the wisdom of this monarch who could realise that the assertion of the right of the state would not be challanged so long the effected persons were not reduced to poverty and exposed to privations.

Turning to the position of the *iqtadars* we find that Ala-ud din allowed them to continue. The power and scope of their exploitation depended on the distance of their postings from the capital. Thus the outlying provinces like Gujarat, Malwa, the Punjab, Awadh, Bihar and Bengal were hardly effected by his reforms, the only difference now being that they were required to remit the surplus to the imperial treasury. The extent to which the *iqtadars* of the outlying provinces enjoyed freedom can be judged from the manner in which Ghazi Malik could put pressure on Rana Mal Bhatti of Abuhar to give his daughter in marriage to his brother Rajab.[6] The sudden demand for the annual tax by Ghazi Malik and that too in cash certainly does not fit in the normal procedure adopted in Delhi and its envirous and the Doab region.

Ala-ud-din as a practical administrator fully realised that implimentation of reforms covering the entire territories of his empire was not feasible. He, therefore selected the tract which he could control from Delhi and which constituted the core of his empire as the region on which the reforms should become operative. According to Barani, The villages around the capital, the towns and district in the Doab, from Bayana

5. Tripathi, R. P., *Some Aspects of Muslim Administration*, (1936), p. 256 (Henceforth, simply Tripathi).
6. Afif, *Tarikh-i-Firuzshahi*, Bib. Ind. Text, pp. 37, 38 (Henceforth, simply, Afif).

to Jhain, from Palam to Deopalpur and Lahore, all the territories of Samana and Sunam, from Rewari to Nagore, from Kara to Kanodi and Amroha, Afghanpur and Kabar and whole of Katehar were placed with regard to payment of revenue subject to one standing regulation of measurement.[7] The account of Barani is rather involved and it seems he did not care to check up the names of the places he was mentioning. In the absence of notes or documents he was most probably writing from his memory in the sequence as they came to him. However, with all its limitations it provides us with some data and enables us to have an idea of the extent of the territory over which Ala-ud-din's revenue reforms became operative. The list as it stands includes a fairly large area, and according to Moreland it covers the centre of the kingdom and omits the outlying provinces.[8] In this connection Dr. Tripathi remarks : "The entire liower Doab in the United Provinces, Oudh, Gorakhpur, Bhar, Bengal, Malwa, Western Punjab, Gujrat and Sindh were left out. Bengal was practically independent, Gujrat and Malwa had not been fully subdued. 'Gorakhpur and the Tarai were yet *terra-incognita.* But it is difficult to say why Oudh and the eastern and central parts of the modern United Provinces were not included."[9]

To impliment the reforms Ala-ud-din had to reorganise the revenue department. He tried to infuse vigour into the existing organisation and insisted that the officers discharge their duties honoestly. The overall charge of the finanee department was with the *wazir*, but Ala-ud-din showed preference to military commanders for appointment to this post Khwaja Khatir who was allowed to continue as *wazir* at the time of his accession was replaced by Nasrat Khan within a year. Nasrat Khan, however, soon became unpopular because of his being too oppressive and had to be transferred

7. Barani, p. 288
8. Moreland, p. 34
9. Tripathi, p. 265

to Kara. Next incumbent seems to have been one Sayyid Khan about whom we hardly get any information. Finally we find Malik Kafur holding the office of *wazir* as well as that of *Naib-i-Sultan*. Appointment of Military commanders as wazir no doubt enhanced the prestige of the office, but prevented the wazir to devote full attention to the working of the department, and, as a result *Naib-i-wazir* had to carry out the plans and supervise the actual working of the department. Immediate assistant of the *Naib-i-wazir* was the *mushrif-i-mumalik*. Jalalud-din Khalji in his desire to give a position in the *wizarat* department to one of his relations had created the office of *waqoof* and this office continued after him. The *waqoof* looked after the expenditure side and the *nazir* supervised the income side. Both these officers worked directly under the supervision of the *mushrif-i-mumalik*. Besides these officers, there was also the *mustaufi-i-mumalik* who acted as 'Auditor General'. In the sub-divisions or the parganas the *mutasarrif* or *amil*, the *mushrif*, the *muhassil*, *gumashtas*, *sarhangs* and *nawisandas* (writers) were officials directly connected with revenue work.[10]

Ala-ud-din realised that without correct assessment of the produce, government would not be in a position to determine the exact amount that was due to it as revenue. Under the existing system the *iqtadars* and the middlemen kept with themselves a major share while they extracted from the peasantry as much as they could. Ala-ud-din's first step to improve matters, therefore was to introduce the system of measurement as the method of assessment, which would enable the government to ascertain exactly the extent of cultivation. Assessment of revenue on the basis of measurement was neither new to the Turks nor was it an innovation for the Indians. It had already been in existance in Persia when the Turks entered that region. Similarly there is ample evidence to indicate that the system prevailed in India

10. Barani, pp. 288, 289

prior to the coming of the Turks.[11] But after the occupation of the norhern India by the Turks, the system had been given up as it required an elaborate machinery and proper vigilence which the new conquerors were not in a position to muster.

According to Barani, Ala-ud-din ordered that the revenue should be uniformly realised on the basis of measurement indicating the actual area sown with the produce of a *biswa* as the unit of measure.[12] The actual words of Barani require some explaination. He mentions that the revenue was to be collected on the basis of : *ba hukm masahat wa wafa-i-biswa.* In this phrase the word *masahat* has been used as a technical term,[13] indicating the system of measurement. According to Moreland, it is an early synonym for *jarib* or *paimaish,* which term became more common during the Mughal rule. The word *masahat,* however, does not seem to have been completely forgotten, it was but rarely used because the more complex *zabti* system operated in which *zabt* and *jarib* were usual terms. The phrase *wafa-i-biswa,* according to Moreland, has also been used in the technical sense with which Barani was familiar, and carried the sense of yield per *biswa.*[14] The word *wafa* carrying a sense of ability to bear, most probably, entered into the revenue terminology indicating the load that a *biswa* was able to carry *i.e.* yield or produce. The whole phrase indicates the system of measurement for assessment of revenue in which the produce of a *biswa* was taken as unit for calculating the total revenue. The other term used by Barani is *hasil* which connotes sharing for which later on *ghalla bakhshi* or *batai* began to be commonly used. The use of the term

---

11. For details see : U. N. Ghoshal, *The Agrarian System in Ancient India,* Calcutta University Press, 1930) ; Tripathi, R. P., *Some Aspects etc.*, p. 161 *notes* 204, 205.
12. Barani, p. 288.
13. Wilson's Glossary defines the word as measuring, measurement : whence the Telgu *Mashatu,* measurement of land, survey. *Glossary*, p. 333.
14. Moreland, p. 226.

hasil indicates that the other system, operating in such places where *masahat* could not be enforced, was sharing.

The system of measurement as given by Barani does not explain many of the aspects connected with it. The first question comes about the standard of measurement *i.e.* the actual area in terms of yards or meters indicated by the *biswa* of Ala-ud-din's time. Secondly, the process adopted to determine the produce of the *biswa* which was to serve as the unit of measure. It certainly could not have been implied that the produce of the *biswa* was determined after the harvest, for in that case the whole idea behind measurement becomes meaningless. Besides, we find that Ghiyas-uddin discontinued this system as it did not take into consideration '*bud wa nabud*' *i. e.* crop failure and was considered as an innovation leaving ample scope for speculation. Could it be possible that the produce of the *biswa* had been fixed by the Sultan on the basis of some data which is not available to us ?

After fixing the method of assessment Ala-ud-din turned to the agencies of revenue collection, with which he was vitally concerned. He was convinced that the rebellious spirit in the various groups including the *iqtadars*, was mainly due to their affluent condition. Beyond a few urban centres "the organised anarchy of the rural intermediaries reigned supreme." The petty Hindu chiefs who had been reduced to the position of village headmen after the Turkish occupation of northern India, continued to offer indirect resistance in the form of "non-payment of taxes, plunder of the trade routes, and sacking the city suburbs and overpowering their neighbours."[15] "The administration which had no local agency, was often reduced to the necessity of collecting land revenue through the army, which the local chiefs did not hesitate to fight ...The government officers at times inflicted hideous and

15. Mohammad Habib, *Introduction*, Elliot and Dowson, ii, p. 73.

unpardonable punishment on the villagers, without making any distinction between the innocent and the guilty."[16]

To curtail the power of this class Ala-ud-din decided to strike at the root of their power He deprived them of their right of revenue collection and made arrangements for revenue collection directly from the cultivators through government staff. The immediate consequence of this step was that the rural areas had to be provided with sufficient staff consisting of *amils mushrif*, *muhassil*, *gumashta*, *navasinda* and *sarhangs*.[17] These officers carried out the work of assesment as well as collection, and, after collection deposited the amount with the central treasury. The intermediaries like *khuts*, *muqaddams* and *chaudharies* now being relieved of the collection work were directly effected. They could no longer shift the burden of their own share of the revenue to the cultivators, besides, they were deprived of the perquisits which they had been enjoying so long as remuneration of their services. These steps certainly hit the financial resourses of the petty chiefs.

Next Ala-ud-din turned to the *iqtadars* who, like the middlemen, were relieved of the work of revenue collection. The revenue was to be collected by the *amil* and his staff, and the collection had to be brought to the central treasury from where disbursements were made.[18] "The establishment of direct relations with the peasants over such a large area," writes Moreland, "must necessarily have involved a rapid increase in the number of officials ; and such an increase was apt to result in an orgy of curruption and extortion."[19] But Ala-ud-din was not oblivious to such possibilities and was not prepared to allow the exchequer to suffer from the venality of the revenue officials. To prevent this he took two positive steps. One, he raised the salaries of the revenue officials so

16. *ibid.*
17. Barani, p. 288.
18. *ibid.*, p. 324.
19. Moreland, p. 35.

as to enable them to live in respectibility and comfort without being forced to resort to corruption.[20] Two, he imposed drastic punishment for bribery and embezzlement. To find out the exact collections Ala-ud-din issused instructions that the *bahi* of the *patwari*, which contained entries of all payments made to each official, was to be compared with the returns of the officials and even for the smallest difference the officicials were to be severely punished and even imprisoned.[21] The employment in the revenue department, as a result of these steps, had so much fallen in estimation, that according to Barani no one would give his daughter in marriage to a revenue official, the office of *mutasarrif* was accepted only by those who had no regard for their lives.[22]

The collection of revenue, with all strictness, possibly could not have been kept up to date. Various factors including natural calamities stood in the way of full realisation of the dues. To keep this arears separate from the current dues, Ala-ud-din created a new branch in the *wizarat* department called *mustakhraj*. "The duties of the *mustakhraj* department were to enquire into the arrears standing against the names of collectors or agents and to realise them."[23]

Ala-ud-din increased the demand of the state share in the produce of the land. Under the new rules the cultivator was required to pay 50% of the produce as land revenue.[24] We have no information about the percentage of the produce demanded by the Sultans prior to Ala-ud-din and therefore, cannot calculate the percentage of the increase. Any statement that prior to Ala-ud-din it was 25% or 33% is based on mere speculation, and in the absence of specific date there can be no end to such speculations. Some scholars have

20. Barani, p. 292.
21. *ibid.*, p. 288.
22. *ibid.* p. 289.
23. Tripathi, p. 218.
24. Barani, p. 287.

qualified this demand by saying that it was on the gross produce and when calculated on the net *i.e.* after deducting the cost of investment in the shape of seeds, impliments and labour of the cultivator it would come to much more. Added to this the grazing tax and the house tax the cultivators were paying as much as 75% to 80%. However, in this connection one may point out that in rural taxation when demand was made on the produce and not on the land it was always on the gross. Besides, the calculation or the idea of the net produce is an outcome of economic theories of modern times and which was beyond the conception of medieval mind. Ala-ud-din who had full knowledge of the exploitation by various groups took measures to prevent the exploitation not for the benefit of the cultivators but for himself. When he raised the incidence of taxation and made the payment direct, he was actually appropriating to himself what previously was the gain of the intermediaries. It can not, however, be stated with certainty whether the demand of 50% which is the highest point sanctioned by the Islamic law was fixed in observance of the law or it was merely a coincidence or judicious thinking that beyond this point the peasantry would not be able to bear the burden. The peasants do not seem to have been materially effected much, at least such a conclusion one is tempted to draw from the fact that neither revolts not dessertions took place after the imposition of this enhanced rate. The cultivators, however, it may be suggested, derived an indirect satisfaction when they saw their erstwhile oppressors being subjected to the same treatment which they had been suffering so long from them.

Regarding the mode of payment, we find that Ala-ud-din preferred payment in kind. According to Barani, the Sultan ordered that in the entire *qasbas* of the *khalsa* and the Doab, the revenue should be collected in kind, whereas in *shahar-i-nau* (the eapital) and its adjoining territories at least half of the revenue should be collected in kind.[25] The collection of

25. *ibid.*, p. 306.

revenue in kind during the first quarter of the fourteenth century definitely relieved the cultivators from the resposibility of converting their produce into cash for payment of revenue and must have been a relief as it protected them from the vagaries of price fluctuations and prevented them from falling into the clutches of village *sahukars*.

Besides land revenue, Ala-ud-din collected *karahi* house-tax) and *charai* (grazing-tax). The term *karahi* or *gari* if it is accepted to indicate house-tax begs another question. Was this tax applied to the urban area or rural area or to both ? In India we know the rural areas hardly had any house except huts, and a structure which could be called a house belonged only to the headmen *i.e. khuts*, *muqaddams* and *chaudharis* and some of the petty chiefs. This class certainly was in a position to pay this tax. Thus the burden of house-tax on the peasantry is doubtful. The grazing tax also needs examination. The grazing-tax would effect those who kept cattle and in rural areas almost every one had some cattle. Thus the burden of this tax was certainly to be borne by the villagers. In Islamic law a *nisab i.e.* taxable minimum had been provided for. Our difficulty comes from the fact that *nisab* is indicated in relation to *zakat* tax. The *zakat* was a religious tax for which minute regulations had been laid down by the jurists. The first important condition being that the tax could not be valid unless the payee understood its significance and possessed free property. Because of this qualification infants, lunatics, slaves, debtors, insolvents and non-Muslims were exempted from its payment. The jurists laid down different *nisab* for different kinds of property. For camel the *nisab* was fixed at five, for buffalos at thirty and sheep and goat at forty.[26] The main consideration in levying the *zakat* was that it should not be charged on the primary necessaries of life. Barani does not speak of any *nisab*, Firishta writing in the seventeenth century mentions that animals upto two pairs of oxen, two buffalos, two cows

26. Tripathi, p. 346 ; *Hedaya*, Tr. C. Hamilton, i, pp. 10-14.

and ten goats were free from levy of tax.[27] Scholars[28] have inadvertently mixed up the statement of Barani and Firishta and have expressed their view that the exemption mentioned by Firishta is doubtful because Barani is silent on the issue. But actually the statement of the two, Barani and Firishta, refer to two different taxes. Barani speaks of *charai*-pasture or grazing tax, while Firishta speaks of the *zakat* on the cattle. Barani's account becomes more clear if we bear in mind that the tax was levied on all wet animals, which implies that the dry ones were exempted from the payment of this tax. He is not talking about the cattle tax. The incidence of the *charai* fell on the non-Muslims and the Muslims alike, but the *zakat* applied to the Muslims alone. Dr. Tripathi on the testimony of Ibn Batuta expresses the view that "Ala-ud-din abolished the cattle tax."[29] But Firishta, it seems found from some source, which he does not mention, that Ala-ud-din did not completely abolish the *zakat* on the cattle but modified the *nisab* slightly than what had been allowed by earlier jurists.

Thus we find that Ala-ud-din's revenue policy was comprehensive enough to take into account all aspects connected with revenue. The revenue department was improved and mal administration was removed. The revenue officials were brought under proper control ; balancing of their returns with the *bahi* of the *patwari* served as an effective check on their mal practices. The middle-men lost their importance and had to undergo financial loss. The rural areas for the first time felt the impact of the Turkish rule. His revenue policy effected the Hindus as well as the Muslims. While the Muslims suffered corporal punishment the Hindus suffered financial loss. Their affluence was gone. the *khutus*, *muqaddams* and *chaudharis* were deprived of their resources for

27. Firishta, i, p. 109.
28. Tripathi, pp. 263-64 ; K. S. Lal, *History of the Khaljis* (1967), p. 183.
29. Tripathi, p. 264.

offering resistance. But the statement of Barani that the wives of the *khuts* and *mugaddams*, because of poverty, were forced to seek jobs in the houses of the Musalmans and earn their wages[30] is rather absurd. It is an outcome of his personal hatred for the Hindus and is far remote from the truth. The *khuts* and *muqaddams* lived in rural areas where the Muslim population, if it existed, hardly had the means beyond keeping a few cattle and some earthen pots and lived, from hand to mouth. The affluent lived in the urban areas which by itself eleminates the possibility of women daily coming from rural areas to serve in the houses of the residents in the urban locality. Besides, the *khuts* and the *muqaddams* at no stage of Indian history ever reached that stage of poverty. This is only one of the many typical examples of hyperbolical expression with which our Persian chronicles abound.

30. Barani, p. 288.

6

Significance of the Accession of Firuz Shah Tughlaq

The accession of Firuz Shah at a place far remote from the capital and under dubious circumstances is yet another aspect of medieval Indian history which deserves re-examination. The question of his accession becomes all the more intriguing because we find Firuz Shah was not the only male surviving member of the house of Tughlaq Shah and we also know that the claims of two other candidates were actually put forth by two different groups. Thus his accession could not have been without some meaning in the context of contemporary political atmosphere. The questions whether Firuz was an usurper or a legal successor, or, whether Muhammad bin Tughlaq was survived by a son have been already examined by various scholars.[1] Here we are not concerned with these aspects, though they might be taken up in some other context. Our main concern in the present paper is to examine the considerations that contributed to the elevation of Firuz to the throne and the consequences of these considerations on the future policy of Firuz Shah as well as that of the State.

Mohammad bin Tughlaq by his actions and policies had antagonised a major section of the nobility and had turned the *ulama-mashaikh* group into bitter enemies. Yet his personality was such that these hostile elements with their constant efforts failed to dislodge him from his authority. His sudden death at Sonda in Thatta on March 20, 1351 (21, Muharram, 752), therefore came to them as a pleasant surprise. It also provided them with an opportunity of having a monarch to their own liking. The burden of the entire narrative of Barani and Afif of the circumstances leading to the accession of Firuz Shah is that, the Mongols who were

---

1. Sri Ram Sharma, *Studies in Medieval Indian History*, pp. 139-45 ; Mahdi Husain, *Tughlaq Dynasty*, pp. 385-92 ; J. M. Banerjee, *History of Firuzshah*, pp. 18-25 ; R. C. Jauhri, *Firoz Tughlaq*, pp. 8-31.

present in the camp of Muhammad bin Tughlaq as his allies began to plunder the camp on learning about the demise of the Sultan.[2] Barni says that Firuz Shah in consultation with the *amirs* rewarded the mongols and permitted them to return to their own country.[3] The first doubt regarding the circumstances of his accession comes from the fact that Firuz Shah who was not the head of the state called the amirs for consultation and granted permission to the Mongols to depart. But when the Mongols pitched their tent a few miles away and began to harass the Imperial camp, Firuz Shah did nothing to prevent them from their activity. Barani and Afif both mention that there was complete confusion in the camp after the death of the Sultan. The description of the confusion when read in the context of future selection of Firuz as king reveals that both these chroniclers have suppressed the truth under the garb of confusion. Truely speaking the confusion as mentioned by these chroniclers refer to the negotiations that took place between different groups in the camp regarding the decision to be taken in respect to (i) the person to be selected, (ii) whether the announcement and final decision was to be taken then and there or later on after reaching the capital.

These leaders could not arrive at a decision all at once and the delay caused confusion in the camp followers and the soldiers as they could not understand who would be the new king or which group would finally succeed in setting up its candidate. Our difficulty is chiefly due to the versions of Barani and Afif, which were unsuspectingly copied by later Persian historians. Barani who was writing to please Sultan Firuz Shah so as to get financial assistances to lead the same comfortable life to which he was habituated, deleberately

2. Ziauddin Barani, *Tarikh-i-Firuzshahi*, Bib. Ind. Text., (henceforth referred as Barani) p. 532 ; Shams Siraj Afif, *Tarikh-i-Firuzshahi*, Bib. Ind. Text., (henceforth referred as Afif) p. 44-51.
3. Barani, p. 533.

introduced many things in justification of Sultan Firuz Shah's accession and he is certainly guilty of suppressing the truth.

The selection of a successor was not an easy task because Muhammad bin Tughlaq was survived by quite a number of persons whose claims were atleast equally as strong as that of Firuz if not more. Among the male members of his family he was survived by his brother Mubarak Khan[4], his nephew (sister's son) Dawar Malik,[5] his two grandsons Muhammad and Maudud[6] (sons of his daughter) his son who was a minor and his cousins (sons of his uncle Rajab) Ibrahim bin Rajab, Qutbuddin bin Rajab[7] and Kamaluddin (Firuz) bin Rajab. Thus we find that if the desirability of keeping the crown confined to the house of Tughlaq Shah was deemed necessary by the contemporaries, they were provided with a sufficiently wide range of persons from whom any one could be picked up for the throne.

The persons who were interested in the succession of a new monarch were divided into different groups each with a marked interest of its own. One group consisted of the military commanders who had accompanied Muhammad bin Tughlaq in his campaigns in Sindh. Another group also belonged to the camp of the late Sultan though numerically in a very small minority. The third group consisted of the *Mashaikh* who felt agrieved by the strong measures taken against them and to this group the ulama also attached themselves as they sensed danger to their own interest in the accession of a strong monarch. The fourth group consisted of administrator-politicians who controlled the capital and

4. *Rehla* of Ibn Batutta, p. 78 ; Barani, p. 527 ; Barani includes him as a courtier of Firuz Shah.
5. Barani, p. 527 ; Afif, p. 45.
6. Afif, p. 419.
7. Firuz Shah after his accession appointed Ibrahim bin Rajab as *Barbak* and Qutbuddin as Amir-ul Umara, vide Mahdi Husain, *Tughlaq Dynasty*, p. 393, n. 3.

from there pulled the strings of administration. The consideration before the first group was the desirability of having a person of mild temper with abilities who could provid them with some leadership and yet be not so dominating a personality as to act as an autocrat. The second group was governed by their interest of raising somebody to the throne with a show of legality who would reward them in return. The third group was interested in having a monarch who would compensate them for their sufferings in the past regime and submit himself to the dictates of religion or things practised in the name of religion and thus provide a comfortable living to the *Mashaikh* and the *ulama* and thereby indirectly allow them to dictate the policies of the state which as a class they believed was their right and from which they had been deprived of by rulers like Ala-ud-din and Muhammad bin Tughlaq. The fourth group was interested in the continuity of the poliey of Muhammad bin Tughlaq in which course they discovered the contnuity of their own authority.

Barani and Afif both have described the character of Firuz Shah, pointing out at the same time, the candidate of the second group as incompetent and by casting doubt about the legality of the son who was set up by the fourth group. They are quite silent about other persons who too had claims on the throne. This silence was certainly not due to their ignorance about them because they do mention them later on in the reign of Firuz Shah. The silence indicates that since their cause was not sponsored by any group, therefore, they could not come into the story they were relating. Thus it will be worth analysing the factors that possibly could have recommended Firuz to these groups. In backing Firuz they seem to have been influenced by the character of Firuz than anything else. In the character of Firuz they discerned all the requisite qualities which would enable them to achieve their ends.

An analysis of the character and personality of Firuz will reveal that he was a typical product of the age, ambitions and yet shrewd enough to wear a mask of disinterestedness. Capable of assuming false appearance of virtue of goodness with dissimulation of real character, he posed as leading a religious life with constant proclaimation of his championing the cause of Sunni orthodoxy. That he was addicted to liquor from early in his life can be noticed from the incident of his marriage with the sister of Saharan and Sadhu.[8] So far his ability as a military commander is concerned it becomes doubtful in view of the fact that Muhammad bin Tughlaq never assigned to him any task in which his military ability was to be taxed. Yet we find both Barani and Afif stressing the point that military commanders in the imperial camp at Thatta selected Firuz because in distress they felt that he was the only person capable of taking them back to the capital with safety. Surprisingly enough we are not told how all of a sudden Firuz came to be recognised as a military leader. Besides, if it was merely a question of bringing back the camp to the capital why could he not be elected only as the commander of the army. Why was it felt necessary to elect him as Sultan and get his coronation done in a far off land ?

If we read in between the lines of the narrative of the two chroniclers we will find that consideration for such a course of action was different than what it appears to be. While the *ulama* and the *mashaikh* were negotiating with the military leaders about the candidature of Firuz, Khudawandzada, daughter of Tughlaq Shah and mother of Dawar Malik, sent a message to the nobles urging that "it was not proper to prefer the *Amir-hajib* to her son, seeing that she was daughter of Sultan Tughlaq, and sister of Sultan Muhammad. Whilst her son lived, how could any stranger sit upon the throne.[9] The stand taken by Khudawandzada created a problem for those who had planned for the accession of Firuz. Besides, Khudawandzada had raised the issue of legitimacy by claiming nearer relationship of her son to the late Sultan. The

8. *Mirat-i-Sikandari*, (Baroda), p. 7.
9. Afif, p. 45.

leaders of the first group thought it advisable to settle the issue amicably and as Afif tells us, the Maliks and the Sufis sent Malik Saifuddin Khoju (Khwaja) as their messenger to negotiate and convince Khudawandzada the desirability of withdrawing the claims of her son in favour of Firuz. Afif mentions that Khoju argued with her that her "son was an incompetent person, incapable of governing. We have come into this foreign country, and a large Mughal army confronts us ; if thou wishest to save theyself from that army do thou acquise in what we all have determined, and the office and the title of Firuz *i. e.* Naib Barbak shall be conferred upon thy son".[10]

The negotiations clearly indicate that the supporters of Firuz were in a majority but at the same time the supporters of Khuawandzada were not such a minority as to be completely neglected. Thus a bargain had to be struck or an offer had to be made to appease her and her supporters. It was the desirability of a joint venture that was stressed though outwardly the garb of Mongol threat as immenient danger has been put forth. The rivalry in a far of place was recognised by the groups as detremantal to their interest.

Barani and Afif both try to make us believe that the kingship was imposed upon Firuz who was not at all interested in having it. According to Barani, "When the anxiety of the army reached its limit and people began to feel that the destruction of their own lives and property as well as those of their women and children was almost in sight and the cries of dismay arose on all sides, Makhdumzada Abbasi, Shaikh-ul-Shuyukh Misri, Shaikh Nasiruddin Mahmud Awadhi (Chiragh-i-Dehli), Ulama, Mashaikh, Maliks and Amirs and respectable persons and leaders of every group collected in a body and agreed to elect Firuz as the Sultan. They then went to the camp of Firuz and presented to him with one voice : 'Thou art the heir apparent and legatee of the late

10. *ibid*, p. 46.

Sultan : Thou art the son of Tughlaq Shah's brother : Sultan Muhammad had no son, and there is no one in the city (Dehli) or in the army enjoying the confidence of the people or possessing the ability to reign. For God's sake save these helpless people ; ascend the throne, and deliver us and many thousand other miserable men ; redeem the women and children of the solidiers from the hands of the Mongols and earn the blessings of two lakh people. Sultan Firuz begged to be excused but the leaders of the state and religion did not listen to his pleadings.[11]

According to Afif , "The nobles of Sultan Muhmmad Shah assembled in council, and after a long and debated deliberation, the nobles and the administrative officers both agreed that proper course was to place the reins of administration in the hands of Firuz Shah. Firuz Shah through fear of God, was averse to being made king and stated that he had formed the plan of making the pilgrimage to Macca."[12] Not withstandlng the decision of the leaders upon choosing Firuz as the new king he continued to be hesitant and would not give his consent. "Tatar Khan who was the leader of the meeting," says Afif, "then stood up, and taking the arm of Firuz Shah forced him to sit upon the throne."[13]

The reluctance of Firuz Shah to accept the throne is quite significant. Was he really disinterested in becoming a Sultan ? On the contrary, if we closely examine the narraives we will find that he was very much interested in acquiring the throne. His reluctance or hesitation was the result of his uncertainty regarding the support that he would get from all sections of the kingdom. In spite of the assertions of Afif and Barani the sections that were supporting him were only a fragment of the officers of the state who were present in the camp of Sultan Muhammad bin Tughlaq.

---

11. Barani,. pp. 535-36.
12. Afif, p. 44.
13. *ibid.*, p. 46.

The officers in other parts of the kingdom had not been consulted and Firuz was quite conscious of it. Therefore by showing his reluctance he was trying to judge his strength of the support. One may agree or disagree with the view that "all talk of Firuz Shah's reluctance........seems to have been the result of publicity manager's imagination........"[14] but one thing is certain that reluctance was not an indication of his real desire. He was very much interested in becoming a sultan and did manage things in such a way as to achieve success. He had negotiated with Shaikh Nasiruddin Mahmud Awadhi *Chirag-i-Dehli* who was recognised as the leader of the Mashaikh group. Another reason which might have prompted him to show his reluctance was to learn the re-action in the capital. He certainly must have known the departure for the capital of Malih Tuntan,[15] the slave of Khawaja-i-Jahan, who had been sent to the royal camp by the wazir, and by showing reluctance he wanted to gain some time. In the mean time by showing his indifference to the things happening and by not taking any measures to prevent confusion in the camp after the death of the sultan he actually created a situation in which the nobles of the army were forced to take a decision so as to end the confusion that prevailed in the camp. Is it not worth noting that during the interval of the death of Muhammad bin Tughlaq and his accession he did not take any step to prevent the Mongols from attacking when he had granted them permission to depart from the camp and immediately after his accession stopped them from their activity.[16]

While discussions and negotiations were going on in Thatta for the accession of Firuz Shah, the news of Sultan Muhammad bin Tughlaq's death reached the capital. This

---

14. Sri Ram Sharma, *Studies in Medieval Indian History*, p. 143 ; see also R. C. Jauhri, *Firoz Tughlaq*, p. 12.
15. Afif has Tuntun. Elliot III, p. 1. Suggests the name as Malih Altun.
16. Afif, pp. 48-49 ; Barani, p. 536.

news was carried by Malih Tuntun who could have reached the capital only after the accession of Firuz Shah which took place three days after the death of the late Sultan and it must have taken quite a few days for the fastest currier to reach Dehli from Thatta. When Malih Tuntun had left Thatta the decision of the nobles was not yet declared, and, may be the negotiations were still going on and Malih Tuntun might have informed the affairs to Khwaja-i-Jahan. The versions of Afif and Barani leave ample scope for doubt. Afif has given two versions. First he says that when Khawja-i-Jahan heard that Sultan Muhammad Shah was dead and that Firuz Shah had been chosen by the nobles and chief men to succeed him, he set up the son of the late Sultan in opposition at Delhi, and gained the people over to his side.[17] But subsequently he mentions that he heard a different version from Kishwar Khan which in reality was correct. According to this versoin when Malih Tuntun informed Khwaja-i-Jahan, he was agrieved at this news and mourned for both Sultan Muhammad and Firuz. Believing the news to be correct he placed on the throne a son of Sultan Muhammad.[18] It is obvious that in his revised version Afif is trying to absolve Khwaja-i-Jahan of any malice against Firuz Shah, or, may be he is trying to justify the accession of Firuz as an outcome of election by the consent of every one and the opposition of the Wazir as only an outcome of his ignorance of the actual proceedings. Khwaja-i-Jahan by raising a son of the late Sultan to the throne raised the legal issue of legitimacy and hereditary succession. Besides, Khwaja-i-Jahan was not alone, he had with him Khan-i-Jahan Qiwam-ul-Mulk, Malik Hasan, Malik Hisam-ud-din Uzbak, Malik Khattab and others.[19] Khwaja-i-Jahan's action no doubt was apparently a move to set up the claim of legitimacy, but the son being a minor the regency was inevitable, which in reality meant the rule of

---

17. Afif, p. 50.
18. *ibid.*, p. 52.
19. *ibid.*, p. 50.

Khwaja-i-Jahan which in its turn implied the continuity of the policy of Muhammad bin Tughlaq with which he was known to have been closely associated. We have already mentioned that the *Ulama* and the *Mashaikh* and the nobles wanted to bring to an end the policy of Muhammad bin Tughlaq and hence opposition to Khwaja-i-Jahan's action was inevitable by this group which had set up Firuz as their king. The version that Khwaja-i-Jahan perceived his error when he heard about the accession of Firuz Shah, leaves ample scope for doubt. Did he realise the mistake of setting up a minor son overlooking the other grown up members of the family like the brother of the late sultan or did he commit the error of taking the initiative in a haste without waiting to watch the course of events, or that the Khwaja perceived this error and regretted is only the expression of the historian who felt the action of the Khwaja as correct but in the face of failure could not dare to justify it.

So far Barani's account of the event is concerned, it is hightly inflated and calls for a great deal of weeding out. Barani in his *Tarikh* is out to please Firuz Shah to whom he dedicated his work. He was closely associated with Muhammad bin Tughlaq and Khwaja-i-Jahan the consequence of which was that with the fall of Khwaja-i-Jahan, Barani not only lost his comforts but had to undergo a period of imprisonment. It was during his imprisonment that Barani started writing at the age of 69 years (lunar). After his release he remained neglected and could not secure any stipend though Sultan Firuz was generously distributing them. It was under these circumstances that Barani wrote *Tarikh-i-Firuzshahi* to attract the attention of the Sultan. In his attempt to please Sultan Firuz he introduced many turns and twists into his narrative so as to present a justification for every action of Firuz Shah. He was conscious of the weakness in the accession of Firuz Shah, and therefore to give legal sanction introduces the story of his nomination by Muhammad Tughlaq. He says Muhammad bin Tughlaq before his death, being extremely pleased with the nurshing and attendance of Firuz declared him his heir apparent just before his death.[20] Barani was conscious that he had been closely associated with Khwaja-i-Jahan and that the new government under Firuz was against all that was associated with him, thus to please those in power he introduces the story of that "Myself and many other reliable courtiers of Sultan Muhammad have heard the late Sultan saying that Ahmad Ayaz (Khwaja-i-Jahan) has become useless. He has crossed the age of seventy and is reaching eighty, he is neither capable of movement nor can he ride. His physical weakness is causing hinderance in the work of Diwan-i-Wizarat. Now he is not fit for administrative work. If he retires and starts living in the *khankah* of Shaikh Nizamuddin Aulia he would retain the regard that he enjoys among the people. I feel shy to say this to him on his face, and it would be better if he makes such a request himself. I shall place the Diwan-i-Wizarat under some one who could run it smoothly."[21] That Barani has deliberately introduced this perverted account can be seen by comparing it with the account of Afif who says that when Firuz was summoned to attend his (Muhammad) person in Thatta, Dehli being thus left vacant Khwaja-i-Jahan was sent to the capital from Thatta as the representative of the absent sovereign.[22] Barani repeatedly condemns the action of Khawaja-i-Jahan in setting up the son of Muhammad bin Tughlaq hoping that such a statement would please Sultan Firuz. In justification of Sultan Firuz's policy as compared to that of Muhammad bin Tughlaq, Barani goes to the length of saying that on being asked by the late Sultan on the course of action to be taken to prevent repeated rebellion he advised him to abdicate.[23] Yet a little earlier Barani says that he could not present to the sultan that the cause of rebellion in all directions was the

20. Barani, p. 532.
21. *ibid.*, p. 531-32.
22. Afif, pp. 50.
23. Barani, p. 521.

result of his excessive severity and that if shedding of the blood was suspended for a while better feeling would spring up and mistrust be removed from the hearts of the people. Thus Barani's account of the accession of Firuz Shah is extremely vitiated by his attempt to please Firuz Shah and therefore except for some of the incidents it is hardly reliable.

Some of the statements found in the contemporary and later writings throw sufficient hints that Firuz had entered into some kind of understanding with the group of Sufis, which he seems to have calculated to be useful for his future. Badayuni narrating the events writing after more than two hundred years of their occurance says that Shaikh Nasirud-din Mahmud *Chirag-i-Dehli* had secretly nominated Malik Firuz as Sultan of Dehli while the emperor was away pursuing his war with the rebels of Gujarat, Deccan and Sindh, the nomination was confirmed by Makhdumzada Abbasi. Immediately on hearing this the emperor summoned all the three *i.e.* Shaikh Nasirud-din Mahmud, Makhdumzada Abbasi and Malik Firuz, to his camp at Gondal. When the arrival of the first two was announced the emperor issued orders for their execution. Simultaneously, however, he fell ill into the agony of death and died. As a result the orders remained unexecuted. The emperor had a son who at that time was out on a hunting expedition. Putting him aside treacherously with the assistance of the amirs and maliks Malik Firuz ascended the throne.[24] The statement of Badayuni has been lightly discarded but what it is worth one may judge it in the context of other earlier and contemporary writings. One thing, however, is clear that in northern India such a belief was in currency even after two centuries has passed since the incident took place. Afif in his introduction to his history of Firuz Shah, speaks in a guarded language the understanding between Shaikh Nasirud-din Mahmud *Chirag-i-Dehli* and Sultan Firuz when he says that "After the death of Sultan Muhammad when Sultan

24. Badayuni, (Tr.) Ranking, I, p. 322.

Firuz became king Shaikh Nasirud-din Mahmud sent the following message to Firuz Shah, "Will you do justice to these men or for this handful of poor and dependent I should ask from God for another ruler." Firuz Shah replied to this message "I will deal with them with patience, toleration and justice." The Shaikh then sent the message, that "If you will act so then I too have prayed for you for a rule of forty years."[25] This version very clearly indicates that terms were offered which were accepted by Firuz and in return he was assured of the assistance. Afif, however covers up this contract under the garb of what he calls the fore-cast of Sufis about the succession of Firuz Shah. Thus according to him when Tughlaq Shah was the Muqta of Dipalpur he went to Shaikh Alauddin the grandson of Shaikh Farid-ud-din accompanied by Muhammad and Firuz. The Shaikh in blessing gave 4 yards of cloth to Tuglaq Shah, 27 yards to Muhammad Shah and remaining 40 yards to Firuz Shah. After their departure the Shaikh remarked that all the there would become rulers. Similarly Shaikh Sharfud-din Panipati and Shaikh Nizamuddin Aulia also blessed and force-cast about the future of Firuz Shah.[26] Certainly Afif has very ingeneously covered the whole under the garb of what may casually seem as the accession of a sufi according to the predestined succession determined by their prayers, but we can discern an underlying meaning behind the entire narrative. Not being sure of his position Firuz surely gave an understanding to the sufis that if he becomes the Sultan the lot of the sufis and the ulama would be different than what it was under Muhhmmad bin Tughlaq. Thus we find that the accession of Firuz Shah was brought about by a combination of the ulama, mashaikh and a section of the nobles all of whom wanted to have a sultan on the throne of Dehli who would submit to their will and not act as an autocrat. These groups wanted a ruler under whom they would get maximum advantage from the government. However we

---

25. Afif, p. 29.
26. *ibid.*, p. 27-28.

can not call Firuz an usurper for the simple reason that nothing was defined regarding succession though the Muslim rule by then was established for more than a century and a half. The principles of nomination, election, hereditary succession every thing existed in a fluid state and the only rule that worked was the exigent of the time and the ability of the person to pick up the crown and put it on his head. It was immaterial whether he picked it with the point of the sword or through manipulations.

Though Firuz had his coronation at Thatta but he had yet to occupy Dehli the capital of the Sultanate, which was then under Khwaja-i-Jahan and where the wazir had set up another king. Thus Firuz had to be very careful and calculative in his move. To prove the nobles in the camp that he really meant to act in consulation with them, he held a council to decide the route that they should follow for the return journey to the capital. The council expressed the view that they should proceed through Gujarat route so that the riches of the country of Gujarat might be secured. But Firuz expressed the view that "When Tughlaq Shah marched to the capital he went by way of Dipalpur and by God's favour obtained success, and, therefore, by following the same route God's favour would assist them to reach safely the capital."[27] The logic as given by Afif is hardly credible because Tughlaq Shah was already posted in Dipalpur where as Firuz was in Sindh, but in rejecting the Gujarat route Firuz was acting with caution. He apprehended resistance on the Gujarat route, whereas the route via Dipalpur passed through places which were important centres of prominent sufis. Besides, Firuz had received information about the stand taken by Khwaja-i-Jahan and expected stiff resistance which called for maximum support from the *Lashkar-i-dua*. He kept the information of Khwaja-i-Jahan's settieg up a son of Muhammad bin Tughlak on the throne secret till he reached Multan. According to Afif, Firuz kept this news

27. Afif, p. 57.

secret because the news might discourage the soldiers who had already by then suffered a lot.[28] But the salient point to note is selection of Multan for divulging the news. It is obvious that at Multan he expected to get more support and ovations, which he felt might dispel all doubt from the minds of the solders about the prospects of Firuz's success against the Wazir.

Firuz proceeded with calculated steps to establish that his policy would be different from that of Sultan Muhammad bin Tughlaq. He started by showing his concern for and deference to the *mashaikh*. On his first halt at Siwistan, Firuz displayed extraordinary zeal in visiting the graves of the sufi saints and paid his homage to departed ones. Whether it was an outcome of his genuine feelings or simply an act to strengthen the support of the mashaikh group in his impending struggle against the Wazir, now is any body's guess. But his act of regranting the *waqf* and *inam* grants which had been rescinded by Muhammad bin Tughlaq certainly benifited the ulama mashaikh group of Siwistan who naturally came out with all praise for Firuz Shah.[29] He observed almost the same routine at his next halt at Bhakkar. He visited the graves of all the departed saints and regranted *waqf* and *inam* grants of which the grantees had been deprived of during the reign of the late Sultan. From Bhakkar Firuz Shah moved to Uchh where he set aside the orders of Muhammad bin Tughlaq and restored all the grants which they had enjoyed prior to their cancellation by the late Sultan. At Uchh he made fresh grants to all those who had no means of livelihood He ordered for the reconstruction of the *Khanqah* of Shaikh Jamalud-din and made fresh grants for its maintenance and handed over its management to the sons of Shaikh Jamalud-din. He thus retorted the family of the Shaikh which had been ruined during the previous reign. Thus Firuz Shah by his actions at Siwistan, Bhakkar and Uchh justified his

28. *ibid.*, pp. 55-56.
29. Barani, p. 538.

selection and proved himself benefactor of the mashaikh in contrast to what Muhammad bin Tughlaq had been to them. He thus earned some reputation and while he was still away from Multan he started receiving petitions from the people of Multan, and, not only gave patient hearing to them but granted whatever was sought for in the petitions.[30]

From Uchh Sultan Firuz came to Multan and as at pre vious places he distributed wealth to the mashaikh.[31] From Multan he proceeded to Ajodhan (Pakpatan) where he visited the grave of Shaikh Firidud din *Ganj Shakar* and thus showed his concern for the sufis. Marching thus he reached Sirsa where he received substantial financial assistance from the sarrafs and traders (beqqals) which replenished his resources and enabled Firuz Shah to distribute wealth to his soldiers According to Afif it was declared that the amount thus received would be treated as a loan taken by the government and Imadul Mulk was ordered that the amount be noted and should be returned to those persons on reaching Dehli.[32] Firuz obviously thus secured the support of this group of the financiers whose money would be safe only if Firuz succeeded in overthrowing Khwaja-i-Jahan. At Sirsa another incident took place which has a special significance in connection with the accession of Firuz Shah. Shaikh Nasirud din Mahmud told Firuz that he had through his prayers brought safely the entire Royal entourage but the region from Sirsa onwards lay within the spiritual jurisdiction of Shaikh Qutbud din Munnawar of Hansi and it was in the fitness of things that he (Firuz) should submit himself into his service and appeal to him for his assistance. Sultan Firuz acted accordingly and wrote to Shaikh Munawwar at Hansi almost the words dictated by Shaikh Nasirud din Mahmud. Shaikh Munawwar replied from Hansi that since Shaikh Nasirud-din was entrusting the entourage from that place to his care he was praying to

30. *ibid.*, p. 539.
31. Afif, p. 60.
32. *ibid.*, p. 61.

God to grant success to the Sultan in the matter of his procuring Dehli.[33] Afif's remark that Shaikh Nasirud din did all that to enhance the prestige of Shaikh Munawwar, otherwise both had cordial relations and were disciples of the same *Pir*, is also very significant. By this remark Afif implicitly shows the steps through which Shaikh Nasirud din *Chirag-i-Dehli* was establishing the superiority of the mashaikh. He was not satisfied with his personal influence on Firuz but wanted to use it for enhancing the prestige of the sufis belonging to his fraternity. The remark also throws ample light on the shrewdness of Firuz who knew the extent to which the mashaikh were capable of propaganda which they could use to boost up the cause of somebody or to denounce those whom they did not like. He thus submitted to Shaikh Munawwar only to enlist his support and through whose propaganda (prayer) he was to have an atmosphere of welcome for himself in Dehli. It was not for nothing that Shaikh Munawwar remarked that Dehli would come to Hansi.[34]

Shaikh Munawwar's prayers seem to have worked well, because while Firuz was still on his way to Hansi defection started in Dehli and Khawaja-i-Jahan's party began to break. The first person to severe his connections from the wazir was his assistant Malik Maqbul Khan-i-Jahan. According to Afif the cause of Khan-i-Jahan's departure from Dehli was that when Khwaja-i-Jahan learnt about the secret understanding between Malik Maqbul and Firuz Shah, he planned to imprison his assistant. But Malik Maqbul was allerted while he was coming to Khwaja-i-Jahan and he at once left Dehli with his family-members and retainers.[35] Malik Maqbul moved with haste and reached the camp of Firuz Shah at Ekdar which Firuz Shah later on developed into a town and named Fathabad. The departure of Malik Maqbul completely upset Khwaja-i-Jahan who being convinced that more desertions would take place decided to submit to Firuz Shah

33. *ibid.*, pp. 61-62.
34. *ibid.*, p. 71.

in the hope if he could save himself by surrender. He started for the camp of Firuz Shah against the advice of his partisans and reached the camp of Firuz Shah at Agroha With the presence of Khwaja-i-Jahan in his camp Firuz could feel himself as master of Dehli and Afif says thus the saying of Shaikh Munawwar that Dehli would come to him there turned out to be correct.

The treatment meted out to Khwaja-i-Jahan is also significant. Afif says that Firuz was favourably disposed towards the Khwaja but the nobles in his camp being opposed to it he handed over the case of the Khwaja to them. Firuz certainly wanted to get rid of the wazir for which Malik Maqbul also must have worked in the camp, because in the exit of the Khwaja he could see the prospects of his own promotion as wazir. Firuz too had his finger on the pulses of the nobles and knew that they hated the regime and the system represented by the Khwaja. Thus by handing over the case of the Khwaja to the nobles he was actually getting a thing done by others which was to his own liking, and, at the same time posing to them that he wanted to act according to their wishes and not according to his own. Barani of course is very apologetic and praises Firuz for his liberal attitude in pardoning the relations of Khwaja-i-Jahan and in punishing only a few of his associates who according to Barani were the persons responsible for instigating Khwaja to oppose Firuz. However, if we look closely into the matter we will find that the persons executed were those who were opposed to his accession and Firuz utilised the occasion of the Khwaja's submission to get rid of them. The manner in which the Khwaja was pardoned, removed from his office and granted in *inam* the iqta of Samana and was granted permission to proceed to his new assignment but was subsequently executed on his way to Samana away from the camp of Firuz Shah stinks with the dirty politics. All this was staged to give a mask to the act in the camp where outright condemnation and execution of the old wazir might create a feeling of apprehension in the minds of the camp followers.

After the execution of Khwaja-i-Jahan, being free from all apprehension Firuz continued his march towards the capital with comparative ease. He halted at Hansi and met Shaikh Munawwar and quitely acknowledged some pieces of advice which he knew he was not going to adhere to. From Hansi, Firuz came to Dehli. He entered the city on Thursday, the 25th August 1351 (2nd. Rajab, 752)[36] and ascending the throne had his coronation celebrations which lasted for twenty one days. Thus Firuz Shah's accession was brought about by a combination of *mashaikh, ulama* and nobility through negotiations, manipulations and compromise. Firuz was conscious of his own weak position. He had no claims on the ground of natural succession or nomination. He had no army under his direct control. He had not established his reputation as a military commander through his military exploits in which soldiers under his command had earned *mal-i-ghanimat* (booty). Under the circumstances he had to depend on the support of the elements who had been dissatisfied during the reign of Muhammad bin Tughlaq, and, in return he had to adopt a policy of appeasement towards these groups and keep them pampered by meeting their demands. Of these groups the ulama-mashaikh group was the most dominating one and Firuz had to be very particular not to offend their feelings. By constantly referring to the ulama and proclaiming time and again that his actions were in confirmity with the *shara* he stressed the Islamic character of the state. Thus with his accession the ulama became the dictators in the matter of state policies ; it was so to say the triumph of the Islamic re-actionary tendencies which had been kept under control by monarchs like Alauddin Khalji and Muhammad bin Tughlaq.

The effects of the circumstances under which Firuz Shah ascended the throne were of far reaching consequences. He had to retain his connection with Muhammad bin Tughlaq and yet established that he was not associated with

36. *Tarikh-i Mubarakshahi*, text, p. 123. Eng. Tr. 126.

the things done by his predecessor and so much disliked by a particular group of persons. To meet this situation Firuz Shah adopted a policy of caution and calculation the key-note of which was to act according to the exigency of the time.

In the accession of Firuz Shah the people and officers of the capital had no say and Firuz realised the need of removing all apprehnsions from their minds, win them over, and, restore confidence in them about his good intentions. He was informed that officers and some people of the capital were anxious because large sums were due from them. These sums had been advanced to them by Sultan Muhammad bin Tughlaq for carrying out development work but had been appropriated by them. Khwaja-i-Jahan, to gain their, support, had also distributed wealth to the people after setting up his candidate. All the money lent and the wealth distributed stood in the government books against the names of respective recipients. When the accounts were presented by Fakhr Shadi, the accountant, Sultan Firuz Shah consulted Qiwam-ul-Mulk. Qiwam-ul-Mulk, who was very shrewd, at once grasped the situation and pointed out that a demand for the restoration of these sums would result only in bitterness without actually getting back anything. On being asked how the Sultan should proceed in the matter he advised him to have all the accounts brought into the public court, and there to destroy them in presence of all the people so that they may be relieved of their anxiety. Firuz Shah approved of this advice, and by his direction the relevent records were brought into his court, where they were publicy cancelled.[37] To justify his action, Firuz Shah inscribed in his *Futuhat* :

"Better a people's weal than treasures vast,"
"Better an empty chest than hearts downcast."

This act of Firuz Shah, no doubt, indicated a fresh approach to state policy, but at the same time it also gives an idea of his own anxiety to please the people even at the cost of the

37. Afif, pp. 93-94.

state. From the advice Firuz Shah discovered in Qiwa-mul-Mulk an adviser to his own liking and appointed him Wazir with the new title of *Khan-i-Jahan*.

Firuz Shah next made his pious declaration not to shed the blood of the Muslims. Making such a declaration at a time when blood of Khwaja-i-Jahan and his associates was still dripping from the executioner's axe, was not without purpose. In his *Futuhat*, Firuz Shah points out that in the reigns of former kings the blood of many Musalmans had been shed and many varieties of torture employed, but the Great and Merciful God made him seek for His mercy by devoting himself to prevent the unlawful killing of Musalmans and inflicting of any kind of torture upon them. He further says that these things were practised that fear and dread might fall upon the hearts of men and that the regulations of the government might be duly maintained. Their motto of government being :—

> "If you want to maintain your kingdom, you will have to keep your sword restless."[38]

At another place Firuz Shah says ;

> "Boast not the hundreds thou hast slain,
> To save one life's a noble aim."[39]

Though Firuz Shah has not named any ruler, but we know the severity of punishments inflicted by Muhammad bin Tughlaq. These pronouncements of Firuz Shah were, in reality, aimed at declaration of a policy different from that of his predecessor. These pious declarations were made with the implicit aim of gaining the favour of the people and silencing any opposition or removing any apprehensions that might have persisted in the minds of those who had been directly or indirectly associated with Khwaja-i-Jahan.

Firuz Shah had seen the consequences of the opposition of the ruling class during the reign of Muhammad bin

38. *Futuhat-i-Firuzshahi*, p. 3; Aflf, p. 20.
39. *Futuhat-i-Firuzshahi*, p. 4.

Tughlaq, and his anxiety to rule peacefully, without being called upon to face opposition, he adopted the policy of settling the ruling class by making the posts hereditary. His aim was to create a sense of security and permanency in them and guarantee their continuance. In this he seems to have gone to the extremes, as Afif mentions. "If an officer of the army died he was to be succeded by his son ; if he had no son, by his son-in-law ; if he had no son-in-law by his slave ; if he had no slave, by nearest relation ; and if he had no relations, by his wives."[40]

Besides making all officers and posts hereditary, Firuz Shah reverted back to the practice of granting revenue assignments in lieu of salary to his officers and soldiers. With hereditary succession these assignments acquired permanent nature. The officials of the state no doubt felt happy and satisfied and thought in terms of the continuity of the reign of Firuz Shah in which they found the continuity of their own rights. Thus Firuz Shah obtained his personal comfort security at the cost of efficiency in the administration. Bribery became rempant and the Sultan instead of preventing it, connived at it. He was afraid that any attempt to put an end to this extra income might result in opposition of the officials.

Firuz Shah had also seen the results of the opposition of the ulama. He had fully realised that the policy of Ala-ud-din and Muhammad bin Tughlaq of keeping the ulama-mashaikh group under control necessitated hard work and constant vigilence. He had also seen the mischief that could be created by this group in spite of vigilence and hard work. Besides, he had gained the throne through their support, and being desirous of remaining on the throne with ease and comfort he adopted the policy of least resistance to this group. He knew that so long this group was well provided for and so long the show of subordination of the secular authority to the dictates of the ulama could be maintained, he would have no difficulty to continue enjoying their support. With this intention

40. Afif, p. 96.

he ordered that all such grants which had been confiscated from religious persons during the previous reign for one reason or the other and had been brought under the exchequer should be returned to their former holders on their production of documentry evidence of the grants made to them by different sultans in the past.[41] Besides restoring the cancelled grants he made fresh grants of lands to the ulama and mashaikh and made adequate provision for their comfortable living.

To keep the ulama in proper humour he time and again posed himself as a champion of Sunni orthodoxy, and, on every matter sought their opinion and pre-sanction before actually taking a step. To the ulama this was like subordination of the authority of the sultan to their own. However, it would be going too far to say that Firuz Shah was an orthodox Sunni in his personal life. We know that he was adicted to liquor and in spite of his promise to Shaikh Qutubdin Munawwar of Hansi who admonished him for his taste, he continued drinking, of course like 'a pious person' in privacy.[42] He was also fond of music and encouraged and patronised it by making it a state ceremonial for the occasions *Id* and *Shab-i-Barat* festivals.[43]

Thus the groups who had sponsored and supported Firuz Shah in becoming the sultan of the Dehli Sultanate could find no cause to repent for their choice. They derived the maximum benefit during his reign. Firuz Shah too ruled without any difficulty. Of all the sultans who sat on the throne of Dehli he alone enjoyed a prolonged comfortable reign. But all this apparent peace, comfort and prosperity was at the cost of efficiency. It sapped the roots of administration. His supplication to the ulama only encouraged a group of unscrupulous selfish people to behave arogantly and pose themselves as the custodians of Muslim conscience. All these combined to create a situation in which desintigration be came inevitable.

41. *Futuhat-i-Firuzshahi*, p. 20
42. Afif, p. 146 : The Tatar Khan episode.
43. Afif, pp. 363-66.

7

The State of Medieval Malwa and the Fifteenth Century India

A special feature of the fifteenth century India was the rise of she Provincial kingdoms as the culmination of the process which had set in with the foundation of the Bahmani and Vijaynagar kingdoms. Their certain was made possible partly by local discontent which was fanned by capable Governors who could understand the local currents better than the Sultan sitting at Dehli. The disintegration of the Sultanate of Dehli also showed that the distant provinces could not be held by military force alone. The provincial kingdoms, each having its own internal problems resulting from local conditions, had to frame policies suitable to the situations each was called upon to face. In the present paper an attempt is being made to analyse some the principles evolved in Malwa state in relation to its internal problems and also the principles evolved to settle inter-state relations.

The thirteenth and the fourteenth centuries witnessed the passing of the political power from the Rajputs to the Turks and the process of change naturally involved a lot of clash and conflict. The motivating factor behind the Turkish invasion was primarily political. But the invading Turk was not only a soldier ; he was also a Muslim. He belonged not merely to an army but also to a faith which laid down a code of conduct that decided the contours of his life both as an individual and as a member of the society. A Muslim ruler, therefore, by definition, had to preserve and strengthen Islam. Thus, paradoxically, a politically motivated conquest led to a change in India's State religion. A cynical war of aggression undertaken not to spread the faith but to grab power resulted in estabishing the dominant position of that faith in medieval India. A political conquest took the outward shape of an Islamic conquest of the Hindus, and every act of aggression against the Hindus, either for breaking their resistance or for territorial extension was loudly proclaimed as holy war—*Jehad*. Barani, for example, enjoined a Muslim king "to make a firm resolve to overpower, capture, enslave and degrade the Hindus." "All the strength and power of the king and the holy warriors of Islam" were to be concentrated "in holy campaigns and holy wars" and the Muslims were advised "to risk themselves in the enterprise so that the true faith may uproot the false creed." The contemporary Persian sources abound in such utterances and often lead a historian to deduce that medieval India was a prolonged process of Muslim oppression on the Hindus. The internal history of the provincial kindom of Malwa, however presents a different picture.

The kingdom Malwa, founded by Dilawar Khan Ghuri (Amid Shah Daud) was established on an enduring footing by his son and successor Hoshang Shah. The Gujarati invasion and his captivity almost within the year of his accession made it clear to Hoshang Shah that the danger to his kingdom from the ambitions of the neighbouring powers was more imminent than from his subjects. He realised that the support of only the Muslim section of his subjects would not help him in maintaining his position against his neighbour, and that religion could no longer be used as an inspiring agent to fight aggressive or defensive wars against his neighbours, who except for Mewar, were all Muslims. He realised that in the altered situation the narrow parochial outlook of the ulama and the theologians, as expressed by Barani, if followed would bring only ruin and destruction to his kingdom. He realised that a policy of religious 'apartheid' clashed with the dictates of sound statesmanship. For advice on polity he turned to Sayyid Ashraf Jahangir Samnani, who was not only a sufi saint but had been himself a ruler, and, had practical experience in both aspects of life. As a sufi Ashraf Jahangir belived in the philosophy of '*sulh-i-kul*' and advocated this principle as the basis of state policy.

Sayyid Ashraf Jahangir did not believe in absolute monarchy, and advised that in important matters of state the king must consult good, honest and learned men. The idea behind consultation was to gain an opportunity of weighing the situation and to gain confidence of the officers. "Consultation", he wrote, "may appear as divulgence of secret, but in reality it is the right method of keeping a secret. In consultation the king must listen to all without atonce expressing approval of any of the opinions. He should move in a way that each one of them feel that the king has acted upon his advice."[1] Hoshang Shah accepted the advice of the saint and adopted the method of consultation as a principle in conducting the affairs of the state. In Malwa, consultation and discussion with high officers and prominent persons, and their approval of the action of the king, became a regular practice. However, it is not being suggested here that it gave birth to some regular constitutional body enjoying the right of advising the king. But consultation with the nobles, practised for about a century, became a tradition in the state system of Malwa ; it was considered by the nobles as their privilege and right, and later in the reign of Mahmud Khalji II when any noble was not consulted he expressed his resentment.

The absence of a settled law of succession had been the bane of the Sultanate of Dehli. It not only led to struggle for the throne even before the corpse of the dead sultan was consigned to the grave, but also created anxiety leading to party factions. The Malwa Sultans seem to have been alive to this question and tried to evolve a principle which was given a fair trial in Malwa. Of course hereditary right was the first principle recognised in the state of Malwa. The hereditary right was accompanied by the right of the ruling monarch to nominate his successor. Mahmud I made further improvement by granting the title of Sultan to the prince whom he nominated as his successor. This became an established practice in Malwa, Ghiyas Shah, Nasir Shah and Mahmud II all got the title of Sultan during the lifetime of the father by whom they were nominated to succeed.

---

1. *Maktubat-i-Ashrafi*, (ms. Ashrafi Library), pp. 75a-82a.

The principle of nomination was put to test on two occasions and on both the occasions it was vindicated. The first occasion came when a number of nobles disfavouring Ghazni Khan tried to set him aside after the death of Hoshang Shah : but they failed because a larger section supported Ghazni Khan on the ground of his nomination. The second occasion is even more interesting. Nasir Shah first nominated Shihab-ud-din as his successor ; but when that prince rose in rebellion Nasir Shah rescinded the earlier nomination in favour of Mahmud Shah. The second nomination was taken as final and after the death of Nasir Shah all the efforts of Shihab-ud-din to assert his claim on the basis of earlier nomination proved of no avail. The monarchy in Malwa, as any where else during the medieval age, was considered as a trust given to the king by God which made the king answerable to God alone and not to the people.

Ashraf Jahangir had advised the king to refrain from tyranny : "nothing can be more destructive for the king than persistent and severe punishment and terrorization of the subjects". The principle advocated here was not a new one ; but in its application the sultans of Malwa did not make any distinction between their Muslim and non-Muslim subjects ; and that was a new thing. As a result of this policy of toleration, destruction of temples or harassment of the non-Muslims is not to be found practised in the kingdom of Malwa. Freedom of worship adopted by the state as its policy stands in contrast with the policy of the other contemporary states. A large number of Jain temples flourished in Mandu, Dhar, Ujjain, Mandsor, Hoshangabad and Ashta, where the images of Jain Tirthankars were worshipped freely. That the policy of toleration observed in Malwa attracted the notice of some of the contemporary Muslim rulers is evident from Mahmud Gawan's reference to of Mahmud Khalji as the *muawin-i-zumrah-i-kuffar* or the helper of the infideles. In the administrative machinery of Malwa we find the Hindus occupying important positions ; they were also included in the advisory council of the monarch. For example, Nardeva

Soni and Sangram Singh were treasurers ; *Ray Rayan* Rai Siva Das commanded a section of the army ; Punja Raj was in charge of the Khalsa lands ; and Medini Rai worked as wazir with Salivahana as his assistant. That the Malwa sultans were trying to establish a broad based state can also be gathered from some of the remarks of the historians of medieval India. Firishta remarks about the reign of Mahmud I that "in his kingdom the Hindus and the Muslims lived happily and maintained friendly relations with each other."

The state of Malwa envisaged the protection and welfare of the people as the primary obligation of the state. In Malwa a public hospital was run at the states's expense to afford free medical treatment. This central hospital had two wings ; one, for convalescence and the other, for the insane. A medical laboratory and a store-house of medical herbs, cellect-ed from different parts of the country. had also been provided to the hospital. In this hospital both Ayurvedic and Yunani systems were practised.

It is generally held that Sher Shah was the first ruler who cared for the cultivators, but here in Malwa long before Sher Shah, we find Mahmud Khalji taking positive steps to encourage cultivation. He ordered that no damage to the crop should be caused by the marching armies ; and if it was caused, full compensation from the state treasury was to be given to the cultivators. He also refrained from increasing the revenue demand when agriculture prospered in any part of his kingdom.

In the process of territorial expansion, the Malwa Sultans reduced a numbhr of petty Rajput cheifs ; but, instead of replacing those chiefs by Muslim military commanders, they allowed them to continue in their territories on payment of tribute and acceptance of the suzerainty of Malwa. The Malwa sultans recognised their responsibility to protect the feudatories against aggression from neighbouring kingdoms, and also to settle their mutual disputes. For example, we may refer to the cases of Rai Parhar and Rai Bhanu of Baglana who were protected from the invasions of Mahmud Sharqi of Jaunpur and Miran Mubarak Shah of Khandesh, and, to the settlement of the disputes between Rai Bhoj of Sarguja and the chiefs of Raipur and Ratanpur. The policy of encouraging the Rajputs to settle in Malwa and granting them *jagirs*, added considerable strength to the state of Malwa. The Rajputs whole-heartedly supported the Sultans of Malwa in their military activity and became one of the main stay of the kingdom.

The relations of Malwa with her neighbouring kingdoms indicate that the States had developed some kind of treaty law based on mutual consent by which they tried to resolve their differences, which served as the basis of inter-state relations in India during the fifteenth century. In the treaty that was concluded between Gujarat and Malwa in 1452, it was stipulated that both should respect the territorial boundaries of each other and continue the exchange of presents. The treaty also specified the areas where each could attempt territorial expansion. The kingdoms of Malwa and Jaunpur also resolved their dispute on the question of suzerainty over the small territory of Kalpi by means of a treaty and the terms agreed upon where honoured by both the parties. Similarly by another treaty the Bahmani kingdom settled its conflicts with Malwa. The treaty negotiations in this particular case indicate that the principle of modification in the terms offered was fully recognised and depended upon mutual agreement and also that the envoys negotiating the treaty were vested with powers by their monarchs to arrive at a final agreement and to sign on their behalf. A treaty thus signed was considered as binding and was honoured by the respective monarchs.

In these treaties the peace negotiators while opening the talk pointed out that because of war between the two Muslim rulers the Hindus were benefitted and that if they ceased to fight they might easily establish the light of Islam on all lands. A section of the Ulama and the Mashaikh who looked upon these clashes as detrimental to the interest of Islam in India also advocated the need of some principles which could form the basis of mutual relationship of these states. From time to time they expressed their disapproval of these clashes and pronounced that such a condition would only help the *kafirs* to take advantage of the situation to become strong.

The pronouncement of the Muslim divines of establishing peace among the Muslim States for the betterment of Islam also provided a method to the rulers and intriguers to justify their actions under the plea of religion. To illustrate the point we may take a few examples : The justification put by the dissatisfied *amirs* of Sultan Muhammad Shah Sayyid in inviting Mahmud Khalji to march on Dehli was that their Sultan was neglecting his duty of protecting Islam. Mahmud Sharqi justified has inavason of Kalpi on the ground that Nasir Khan had deviated from the path of the *Shariat*. Similarly when Mahmud Khalji decided to oust Mahmud Sharqi from Kalpi he charged the latter of anti-Islamic activity. Even Mahmud Gawan interpreted Mahmud Khalji's movements towards Deccan as assistance to the *kafirs* in their invasion of Bahmani kingdom. Thus we see that religious plea could as well be adopted to the interest of war as to those of peace.

The treaties mentioned, however were all signed between kingdoms the rulers of which were Muslims. The desirability of peace between the Muslims being advocated, the basis of agreement was reciprocity of the parties concerned the santity of which was deduced from the *Hadis* : "If the enemy submits for peace one should also bend to accept it."[2] The inspiration to respect the words pledged in the treaty was also derived from the Divine Words. These treaties, therefore, indicate that religion so much dominated the minds of the people that religious justification of the action was taken as the accepted norm in politics.

---

2. *Riyaz-ul-Isnha*, p. 94.

As already pointed out, the political needs of the state demanded establishment of friendly relations or extending protection to the Hindu Rajput chiefs. Such a stand, however, brought in juxtaposition two systems. The Hindu system, which believed in the universality of the application of law irrespective of creed and culture, found no difficulty either in seeking assistance or in forming alliances with states which had Islam as their governing creed. The Muslim states, governed by a legal system which theoretically did not regard non-Muslim states as worthy of friendship or equality, found themselves in an odd position *vis-a-vis* the jurists. Under such a condition they tried to justify their actions either by getting a sanction from the Ulama or by referring to some *Hadis* which covertly lent some support to their action. In such cases the deciding factor, therfore, was mutual self-interest and the Divine Law was utilised to the extent to which a specific provision supported their conduct. It is under these conditions that we can explain the Malwa Sultan's assistance to the chief of Champaner against the ruler of Gujarat, or the Bahmani ruler's concluding treaty with the rulers of Telingana and Vijaynagara. The strength of such treaties depended on the postulate of honouring the words pledged. But a pledge between a believer and a non-believer on terms of equality failed to get religious sanction and whenever necessity arose, a sanction of the Ulama could be obtained for breaking the pledge. In such cases the deciding factor, no doubt was mutual interest, but a religious sanction was deemed necessary in either situation.

The decisions, of course, were influenced by political, economic and other considerations but religious justification offered in such cases leads to the conclusion that such a colouring was based on the assumption that Islamic law was more binding on the individual rather than on the territorial groups and, therefore, satisfaction of the individual was a precondition to success.

The advocacy of peace on the basis of religion, however, proved extremely detrimental to the political interest of the state. It provided scope to the disappointed Muslims to raise the slogan of protecting Islam against a regime where the Hindus had any upper hand, the baneful consequence of which one can notice in the state of Malwa where the ascendancy of Medini Rai and his associates in the administration was resented by a group of Muslims who had to work under him. It may be pointed out, however, that Islam visualised a state where the ruling power would be Muslim, and the non-Muslims would be accorded the position of protected people ; hence the Muslims in India could think of themselves only as belonging to the ruling class and their resentment against Hindu ascendancy arose partly from that sentiment. Thus, when such a group raised its voice in Malwa and won over the Sultan to their view, they simply invited the doom of the kingdom. It knocked out the very basis of the policy on which the kindom of Malwa had prospered. It offered to the Gujarati Sultan an opportunity to interfere in the affairs of Malwa and he succeeded not only in relieving the Muslims from Hindu ascendancy but also in depriving the Malwa Government of the services of efficient men. When the overthrown Rajputs looked to Rana Sanga for help, it gave him also the opportunity to interfere in the affairs of Malwa on behalf of the Rajputs. Thus the internal dissention resulting from the appeal to religion only ruined the state of Malwa and brought about its extinction. The ulama of the fifteenth and the sixteenth centuries do not seem to have realised that a "kingdom can be made peaceful with unbelief and justice and not with Islam and tyranny", a view which we find Ali Muhammad Khan boldly pronouncing in the eighteenth century.[3]

---

3. *Mirat-i-Ahmadi*, ii, p. 462. Tr. p. 790.

8

Some Chronicles and Chroniclers of Medieval India

A historian analysing and interpreting the history of India during the medieval period has to depend much for his source material on the histories or the chronicles written by the contemporary or near contemporary writers. In this, a common misconception has become deeply imbeded in our minds. While considering the source material, we take it for granted that source material on medieval Indian history means Persian compositions only. Prior to the coming of the Mughals the persons who wrote these chronicles belonged to the class of scholars devoted to the study of Islamic theology and were commonly designated as *ulama*. No doubt Islam does not recognise an ordained priesthood, but, in practice, the *ulama* derived their authority from their learning. The common Muslim knew little about the intricacies of his creed and therefore the *ulama*, because of their knowledge, became his mentor. They governed conscience and judged conduct. They decided whether a given action squared with the tenets of Islam. The validity of any action depended not on the categorical imperative of social duty but on the verdict of the *ulama*. Thus by the conditioning logic of their position the *ulama* as a class were hidebound by orthodoxy which was further strengthened by their economic position ; they had no independent means of livelihood. Supported by royal patronage or the patronage of the affluent they had nothing except their dogmatic conservatism to justify the fact that they should be so supported. The intellectual outcome of the narrow sectarian orthodoxy of the *ulama* was the production of the chronicles, the accepted sources of medieval Indian history which contain the lines of theological prejudices across the picture painted or distorted in them. We cannot positively say to what extent religion acted as the motive force behind the drama of medieval Indian history or such was only the interpretation of the writers who tried to justify or condemn the actions of the monarchs in terms of Islam. But certainly such is the picture depicted in the Persian chronicles.

Tradition also played an important role in determining the treatment of history by these chroniclers. Prior to the occupation of India by the Turks in Islamic historiography two traditions had developed the—Arab and the Persian. Persian historiography was an outcome of the revival of Persian culture and traditions under the Turks. Under this fresh inspiration Persian language found its patron among the Turkish rulers and governors. The Arabic language was replaced in these Turko-Muslim regions with Persian and in historiography the Arab method of writing history was dispensed with. "The ancient spirit of Persia was invoked to forge a new path and the history of the ages was converted into the history of the kings....The general trend was to plan all historical works on the Persian model and survey the social landscape from the foot of the royal throne and treat the biography of a sovereign as the history of the times."[1]

The *ulama* who wrote these chronicles treated history on the lines on which they had studied *Hadis*. To them study of *Hadis* was indispensible for one who writes history, because these were twins and one without the other would be incomplete. Thus the words and the deeds of the Prophet and the tenets of Islamic code of conduct served to these writers as the yard-stick to measure the actions of a monarch. Their judgement under the circumstances was bound to have a religious bias.

The medieval Indian chroniclers had also evolved a code of conduct in writing history according to which it was obligatory in the interest of piety that when narrating the excellence, the good deeds, the justice and equity of a ruler or of a great man, his failings, vices and evil deeds were not concealed. Such a stand, however, placed the medieval Indian chroniclers in a difficult situation, who mostly wrote to please or expected to get some benifit from his patron, or wrote at the command of the reigning monarch. It is to get out of

1. K A. Nizami, *Some aspects of Religion and Politics in India during 13th century*, p. 364.

such a predicament that they evolved the principle that "if a historian considers it expedient he should speak openly, but if not, he should speak by insinuation, in hints, and in covert and learned allusions."[2] Another historian of the fifteenth century observes that, "the official historian should, by hints, insinuations, overpraise, and such other devices as may come to hand, never fail to express his true opinion, which, while, remaining undectected by his illiterate patron, is sure to be understood by the intelligent and the wise."[3] These methods provided ample scope to the chroniclers to ventilate their personal views and prejudices by mixing them with narrative of the events. The *ulama* tried to glorify Islamic ideals in their writings through such devices.

According to Peter Hardy, the Islamic or the didactic religious framework in Muslim historiography of India was the result of three main trends. "First was an almost exclusive concentration on the deeds of Muslims in Hindustan." For these chroniclers "non-Muslims are as the furniture and properties for the stage on which the drama of the Muslim destiny and the Muslim political achievement in Hindustan is played. The Hindus are not mentioned, for the most part, except as the passive material on which Muslims impose their will. It is the function of the Hindus to provide opportunities for the practice of Muslim virtue."[4] The second aspect was the "Indo-Muslim historians' acceptance of the Muslim world order" and that the "past is observed through religious spectacle" which with determination they tried to strengthen by their writings. "Whatever happens is brought under the categories of Muslim thought whether or not religion is an element in the situation. Of course, this idiom is more dominant in some of the writers than in others." The third was "the religious presupposition of the Indo-Muslim historians.

2. Barani, *Tarikh-i-Firuzshahi*, pp. 15-16, cf. Nizami, Loc. cit. p. 364.
3. Mir Khwand, cf. Nizami, Loc, cit., p. 365.
4. P. Hardy, *Historians of Medieval India*, p 114.

"...With them an ounce of religious truth weighs more than a pound of fact. Sometimes this attitude is expressed in a humble acceptance . . . God alone knows the truth." Medieval Indian chroniclers "are alike in imputing to Divine Decree the final role in the determination of events. . . ." Even when historical personages appear to be acting autonomously and their wishes and decisions appear to explain what happens, investigation will reveal the hand of God in the background."[5]

Thus we find that the handling of the medieval Indian chronicles as source material demands maximum care and caution, and each statement made in these compositions requires analysis before acceptance. Since much of the personal bias and prejudices of the writer is woven into the texture of the narratives, it becomes imperative that one acquaints himself first with the life of the author and then try to interpret the statements made by them. The personality of the author, the conditions and the purpose for which he was writing are as vital informations for understanding the chronicles, as the circumstances and the chracteristics of the period in which he was writing. These chroniclers lived in medieval times with a medieval outlook and one should not expect them to possess the outlook of the modern times. Jagadish Narayan Sarkar has very correctly pointed out, "We cannot reasonably expect to find modern ideas of history in them. Any attempt to judge these histories with the yard-stick of modern historiography is bound to lead to disappointment and, perhaps, unreasonable criticism."

A. MINHAJ-US-SIRAJ JUZJANI

Maulana Minhajud-din Abu Umar was born in a family of ulama in 1193. His ancestors, on both sides, had been ecclesiastics for several generations, and had distinguished

5. *ibid.*, pp. 115-117.
6. *Quarterly Review of Historical Studies*, Vol. iv, Nos. 1 & 2, p 31.

themselves for learning. After the Ghurian occupation of Lahore our author's father Maulana Sirajud-din Muhammad had been appointed as qazi of the army (*qazi-i-askar*) stationed at Lahore. Abu Umar Minhaj lost his father when he was hardly seven. His father, Maulana Sirajud-din Muhmmad, was killed in an affray with robbers when he was going to the court of the Khalifa along with the envoys of Ghiyasud-din Muhammad bin Sam of Ghur. Young Minhaj was brought up under the care of Princess Mah Malik, the daughter of Sultan Ghiyasud-din Muhammad bin Sam. At several places in his work he speaks in terms of much gratitude of the fostering kindness and protection he received while dwelling in that Princess's household. Thus he was fortunate to have a royal care which fully equipped him as a scholar and provided him scope to become conversent with politics which helped him in later life to judge a situation and act accordingly. His training enabled him to be associated with various envoys between 1210 and 1225. However his earliest independent diplomatic assignment came in 1226 when he was sent as envoy by Tajud-din Niyaltigin to bring about an accomodation between himself and the governor of Kuhistan.[1] Minhaj did succeed in bringing about an accomodation, which however, was not acceptable to Tajud-din Niyaltigin. In anger Tajud-din confined Minhaj in the fortress of Safhed in Sijistan. However, in 1226 he was released on the intervention of Ruknud-din Muhammad. By then his native land was infested with the Mangols and after release Minhaj decided to migrate to Hindustan.

Minhaj migrated to India in 1227 via Ghazni and Baniyan and reached Uchh in May 1227. After a stay of about six months he was appointed as superintendent of the Firuzi *madarsa* by Nasirud-din Qubacha, and was also made the qazi of the forces of Ala-ud-din Bahram Shah son of Qubacha.[2] In the following year Sultan Iltutmish led his

1. Raverty, *Tabaqat-i-Nasiri*, p. xxv.
2. *ibid.*, pp. 541-42.

forces to suppress Qubacha who had asumed sovereignty in Multan. Minhaj could distinguish the winning side, he therefore, deserted Qubacha and went over to the Sultan of Dehli. Minahaj was not the person to remain satisfied with small positions in life and for him Multan was no more attractive as it was now reduced to a secondary position. He, therefore, accompanied the returning train of Iltutmish and reached Delhi, in Ramzan 625 (Aug. Sept. 1228).[3]

After reaching Delhi, Minhaj does not seem to have achieved any particular appointment and remained on the look out for an opportunity to impress the Sultan with his abilities. In 1231-32 when Sultan Iltutmish beseiged the fort of Gwalior, Minhaj left Delhi and joined the royal camp at Gwalior. At Gwalior Iltutmish was facing a determined resistance and required all forms of assistance. Thus the arrival of this ambitious scholar prompted the Sultan to muster his services. He was engaged as a preacher to the army, and was required to deliver *tazkirs*. He was required to deliver the *tazkir* daily on first ten days of the months of Zilhijjah and Muharram and three *tazkirs* per week in the remaining months. During the period of seige he is said to have delivered ninety-five such *tazkirs*, which by itself was no mean achievement. *Tazkirs* were religious preachings in which glorious aspects of Islam and the various hardships undergone in the past by the heroes of Islam were presented to enthuse the soldiers in hard times and particularly when they were engaged in war. These discourses were considered useful in boosting the morale of the soldiers and in maintaining unity among them.

His hard labour and ability received full recognition from the sultan and he was appointed *qazi*, *khatib*, *imam* and *muhatasib* of Gwalior and was made responsible for all matters involving *shariat*.[4] Thus at Gwalior he occupied an impor-

3. *ibid.*, p. 615.
4. *ibid.*, p. 620.

tant position with a number of offices combined in him and thereby affording him with ample scope to display his ability. In those days Delhi was the centre of politics and of power thus away at Gwalior, Minhaj was finding himself neglected. Therefore in 1238 when some officers were recalled by Raziya, Minhaj also accompanied them and reached the capital where it seems Raziya wanted to utilise his services in moulding opinion in her favour. She appointed Minhaj as the superintendent of the Nasiriya madrasa in the capital and allowed him to continue in his offices at Gwalior which charge he started discharging through his deputies.[5]

After the deposition of Raziya, Minhaj wrote congratulatory verses on the accession of Bahram Shah.[6] Thus we find Minhaj displayed his ability to sail along with the current and not only succeeded in retaining his position but also received added honours when he was appointed qazi of the capital. In the year 1241 incursion of the Mongols took place and panic spread in the capital. Minhaj was called upon to deliver *tazkirs* to the people to restore confidence in them. In the same year he was appointed qazi of the empire.[7] But Minhaj was not destined to enjoy continuous smooth sailing through the troubled waters of Delhi politics. The Turkish nobles soon started their revolt against Bahram Shah and Minhaj tried to participate in this tussle. He tried to conciliate them. However he failed in his attempt and narrowly escaped with his life on May 9, 1242.[8] Next day the nobles raised Ala-ud-din Masud Shah to the throne and our outhor tendered his resignation from his offices. It is obvious that his resignation was an outcome of his having taken the wrong side and now he was afraid of its consequences. After his resignation he preferred to leave the capital and on Jan. 2,

5. *ibid.*, pp. 643-44.
6. *ibid.*, p. 649.
7. *ibid.*, p. 658.
8. *ibid.*, p. 660.

1243 he started for Lakhnauti where he stayed till the end of 642/May 1245.[9]

It was for nothing that Minhaj had resigned from his posts and decided to proceed to Lakhnauti. He wanted to find out for himself the groups as they existed among the nobles. He had conference and received encouragement at Badaun from Tajuddin Qutlugh, and at Awadh from Qamrud-din Qiran. When Minhaj was at Awadh, Tughan Khan Izzudin bin Tughril the governor of Lakhnauti was raiding Kara and Minhaj joined him at Kara from where he accompanied the governor on his return journey to Lakhnauti. In 1245 Malik Tughan Khan was recalled from Lakhnauti which was given to Malik Tmir Khan Qiran from whom Minhaj expected to get hardly anything so he accompanied Malik Tughan Khan and reached Delhi on July 11, 1245. Minhaj seems to have been in touch with Ulugh Khan because only three days after his arrival he was appointed superintendent of the Nasiriya college and was given full control over its *waqf*. "The qaziship of Gwalior and the Khitabat of the Jama Masjid, all these, were confirmed to the author, according to former grant and Malik Ulugh Khan-i-Muazzam conferred upon the author a special honorary robe and a caprisoned horse, such as no other among his brethren of the same profession had ever received."[10]

It is evident from the subsequent history that Minhaj was closely connected with a section of the nobility. It is also very probable that Ulugh Khan, who was then building up his future, had recognised his ability as a scholar and also as a preacher and had won him over to his side to utilise him in creating an opinion in his favour. Minhaj too must have recognised the future greatness of Ulugh Khan and, therefore attached himself to him. Nasirud-din Mahmud was raised to throne on June 10, 1246. The disaffected nobles had taken all possible precautions in bringing about this change and

9. *ibid.*, p. 663.
10. *ibid.*, p. 667.

Minhaj had given a full account of the steps through which Nasirud-din was placed on the throne which indicated that he was a partisan of this group and had a first hand information of the incidents. With the accession of Nasirud-din Mahmud Ulugh Khan became all powerful and as Ulugh Khan was the patron of Minhaj his days of prosperity also began. Throughout his work he is full of praise for Ulugh Khan. From Ulugh Khan, Minhaj received valuable presents and even succeeded in securing some horses and slaves for sending them to his sister in Khorasan.

Minhaj was appointed *Qazi-ul-Quzzat* on July 31 1251 but with the ascendency of Imadud-din Rihan when Ulugh Khan lost his position Minhaj too lost his office (1253) which was given to Shamsud-din Bahraichi. However, after a period of about two years Ulugh Khan once more became Naib and Minhaj was again appointed as *Qazi-ul-Quzzat*. Thenceforth Minhaj had a smooth sailing and wrote his chronicle *Tabaqat-i-Nasiri* which he dedicated to the sultan. Though we know from Barani that he was still alive in the reign of Balban, he did not write after Shawwal 658, October 1260. May be that things in the capital were taking a shape which he thought it best to avoid writing. Minhaj himself writes : "The accession of the sultan took place in the beginning of the year 644 and that upto the period of this chronicle will be fifteen years."[11]

Tabaqat-i-Nasiri

Minhaj-us-Siraj completed his *magnum opus* in 658/1260 which will be evident from his remark noted earlier. He dedicated his work to Sultan Nasirud-din Mahmud and entitled it *Tabaqat-i-Nasiri* after the name of the Sultan. Dowson, however, suggests that the work was completed in the reign Sultan Balban. For holding such a view Dowson argues : "The eulogistic way in which he always speaks of the successor of Nasirud-din would induce the belief that the work appeared in the reign of that Sultan, and the fact is proved by his more

11. *ibid.*, p. 675.

than once offering up ejaculatory prayer for the continuance of his reign." But we need not be carried away by the expressions of Minhaj because Balban in fact was the real master and Minhaj wished and prayed for his continuance, in which he could feel his personal safety.

Tabaqat-i-Nasiri is a voluminous work having twenty-three sections. It is a sort of Islamic world history starting from the creation of Mankind down to Shawwal 658 H. Of these sections those from seventeen to twenty-three are useful in the context of Indian history and may be noted.

Section XVII	—History of the Shansbaniya Sultans of Ghur upto its conquest by Muhammad Khwarizm Shah in 1215.
Section XVIII	—The Shansbaniya kings of Bamian.
Section XIX	—The Shansbaniya Sultans of Ghazni from Saifuddin Suri to the conquest of Ghazni by Aibak in 1206.
Section XX	—The Muizziya Sultans of Hindustan consisting of accounts of Aibak, Aram Shah, Qubacha, Bahauddin Tughril, the first four Khalji princes of Gaur upto 1226.
Section XXI	—The Shamshiya Sultans of Hindustan from 1210 to 1260.
Section XXII	—Account of prominent nobles, viceroys and governors who flourished in Shasmhiya dynasty.
Section XXIII	—An account of incursions of infidels ; the Mongols, Chingiz Khan and his descendants upto 1259.

As will be evident from the titles of the sections noted above. Minhaj planned his narrative on the basis of persons and dynasties and therefore, events in which different characters participated have been related at more than one place.

This repetition, while it appears as a defect of the work, has some advantages also. The narrative of the same even at different places can be compared and one may draw his own conclusions out of the considerable amount of variety contained in the details of the same event.

The language of Tabaqat-i-Nasiri is very simple. "Written in a plain, unaffected style the language is considered very correct. The author but rarely indulges in high-flown eulogy, but narrates his facts in a plain, straightforward manner, which induces confidence in the sincerity of his statements and the accuracy of his knowledge." In spite of the simple language one can easily discern his scholarship and his command over the language.

Opinion of Scholars on the Merit of the Work.

Raverty :—"This history is one of the most important works with respect to the early rulers of India, and that part of Central Asia upon which all eyes have been lately turned, and are likely to be turned in future...Our author has mentioned the Afghans but once in his History, and that very briefly, but, at the same time most graphically...The Afghans were by no means unfamiliar to our author, and he certainly knew the Ghuris better than any other author known to us, and he shows on that very page that they were a totally different race...In his account of the Shansabanis of Ghur and their dynasties, he simply stands unrivalled, and also in his accounts of the first Mughal invasions of the territories between Hirat and Multan."[12]

Dowson :—"The *Tabqat-i-Nasiri* is held in very high esteem both in India and Europe. Firishta and others refer to it as an excellent work of high authority. Elphinstone mentions it as a work of the highest celebrity, Stewart in his *History of Bengal*, follows it very closely, and considers it a very valuable

12. Raverty, *Tabaqat-i-Nasiri*, pp. xi, xiii.

book...The auther "appears to have been industrious in collecting information from trustworthy persons, and he often mentions his authority for the fact he records...He is disappointing occasionally in the brevity with which he records important matters about which he might have obtained full information."[13]

Habibullah :—"Its value consistes in its first-hand account of the Shansbani conquests in India and the subsequent history of the new kingdom in which the author held high ecclesiastical and judicial offices. He was not only a contemporary, but also an actual participater in some of the events narrated in the work, which consequently, suffers from personal prejudice. He is biased towards the Ghorids and the dynasty of Ilutitmish and in many places conceals facts unfavourable to his patron Ulugh Khan and the sultan Nasirud-din Mahmud to whom the work is dedicated. Although generally correct with regard to facts, he is very sparing in supplying details and in some places makes contradictory statements. Nevertheless, its value as our main original source can hardly be overestimated."[14]

Nizami :—"Minhaj alone seems to have had detailed personal knowledge of the contemporary events he has recorded in his *Tabaqat-i-Nasiri.* Since he had been closely associated with the Ghurid ruling house, his knowledge of the Ghurid family, its traditions and achievements was definitely more comprehensive and minute than that of any other contemporary writer... Besides, Minhaj had a better sense of history... His anxiety to give chronological details and arrange his data in chronological order is an indication of his disciplined mind."[15]

---

13. Elliot and Dowson, ii, p. 264.
14. Habibullah, A. B. M., *Foundation of Muslim Rule in India,* pp. 10, 11.
15. Nizami, K. A., *Religion and Politics etc.*, p. 369.

B. AMIR KHUSRAU (1253-1335)

Abul Hasan, better known as Amir Khusrau was born in 651/1253 in Patiali (District Eta) in an aristocratic family. His father Amir Saifud-din Mahmud occupied high administrative post during the reigns of Iltutmish and his successors. His mother also came from the family of administrators, being the daughter of Imad-ul-Mulk an officer of eminence during the reign of Balban. Thus young Abul Hasan had no difficulty in getting education, and as a young boy he was placed under the care of Maulana Sadud-din Muhammad. He was a precocious child and started composing poems at an early age of eight, and by the time he was twelve he was proficient in the art. He studied extensively the poetry of different Persian poets and drew inspiration from them. Finally he developed a style of his own and became a poet of renown in his own right. His flare for language made him almost a linguist and he mastered Persian, Turki, Arabic and Hindi languages.[1] However, it is rather sad that we cannot definitely say when Abul Hasan took the pen name of Khusrau, though hypothetically one may suggest most probably from his earliest compositions. He became famous as Amir Khusrau his personal name being thrown into oblivion.

In the medieval times a peot depended much on the patronage of some one who could provide him means to survive. Thus while still young Amir Khusrau attached himself to Alaud-din Khishli Khan, nephew of Balban, in the early years of the reign of this monarch. When Balban posted his son Nasirud-din Bughra Khan to Samana, Amir Khusrau attached himself to that prince and his court. The rebellion of Tughril in Bengal compelled Balban to march in person for suppressing the rebellion and while leaving for Bengal he took with him Bughra Khan. Amir Khusrau also accompanied the royal entourage to Bengal. But he, most

1. For full biographical and critical appreciation of Amir Khusrau's literary works. See : M. Wahid Mirza, *The Life and Works of Amir Khusrau*, Calcutta, 1935.

probably, did not like the climate of Bengal and instead of remaing in the court of his patron, he returned to Delhi along with the Sultan.

Balban's court with stern and severe atmosphere could hardly provide a congenial atmosphere to a poet, and Amir Khusrau moved to Multan, where Balban's eldest son Nusratud-din Muhammad (Khan-i-Shahid) had build up a cultural centre and scholars had taken shelter in his court. Discourses of scholars, poetical recitations and music had become a regular feature of his court. Amir Khusrau was an welcome addition to the gathering and Prince Muhammad appointed him as *nadim*. In Multan Amir Khusrau had had the opportunity of the company of several scholars, and one of them was Amir Hasan Sijji. Amir Khusrau remained in Multan with the Prince for about five years.[2] But in 1284/5 the Prince was killed in one of the Mongol raids, and Amir Khusrau was also taken as a captive by the Mongols. However, he managed to escape from the capitivity after a brief period and returned to Delhi to the court of Balban where he recited the elegy that he had composed on the death of the Prince. The Court of Balban witnessed for the first time the force of Amir Khusrau's poetry. The contents and the manner of recitation moved the entire court who could not resist their tears.

During the reign of Kaiqubad, Amir Khusrau became a *nadim* to Malik Amir Ali surnamed Hatim Khan. When Kaiqubad marched towards Bengal to meet his father Nasirud-din Bughra Khan, Hatim Khan was ordered to join the imperial force and Amir Khusrau accompanied his patron. He thus could witness the proceedings that took place between the father and the son. While returning to Delhi, Sultan Kaiqubad appointed Hatim Khan as governor of Awadh and Amir Khusrau stayed at Awadh with Hatim Khan.

Amir Khurau return to Delhi in 1289 to look after his ailing mother. While he was at Delhi, Sultan Kaiqubad

2. Barani, p. 67.

asked him to compose something on the theme of the meeting of the father and the son, as he himself narrates that the Sultan flattered him and promised to give him a big reward which would free him from all wordly cares ever afterwards.[3] Witnin six months (October, 1289) he presented to the Sultan his poetical composition *Qiran-us-Sadain*. This was his first writing on history in the form of poetry and produced under royal command. Ever after this Amir Khusrau remained attached to the royal court.

During the reign of Jalalud-din Firuz Khalji, Amir Khusrau improved his position considerably and was appointed as the keeper of royal library (*mushafdar*) with a salary of 1,200 tankas. A settled life with a handsome allowance gave Amir Khusrau the opportunity to engage himself to his liter ry activity. In the *mahfils* of the Sultan he was addressed as *maikul nudma*. The reign of this Sultan witnessed the blossoming of the genius of Amir Khusrau. For the Sultan he composed a peon called *Miftah-ul-Futuh* The accession of Ala-ud-din Khalji did not deprive him of the royal patronage. He continued as a court poet during the twenty years of the reign of this Sultan and produced a large number of literary works out of which *Khazain-ul-Futuh* (1311) and *Deval Rani Khizr Khan* (1316) are devoted to historical theme. The reign of Qutbuddin Mubarak Shah witnessed Amir Khusrau at the peak of his form. He composed at the request of the Sultan the *Nuh-i-Sipehr* (1318). The usurpation of Nasirud-din Khusrau did not affect him.

The accession of Ghiyasud-din Tughlaq Shah witnessed a change in the dynasty, but Amir Khusrau maintained his position. At the request of the new Sultan he composed the *Tughlaq nama* (1320). During this period he also added some portion to his earlier composition *Deval Rani Khizr Khan*. Amir Khusrau lived long enough to see the accession of Muhammad bin Tughlaq but the death of his friemd and *pir* Shaikh

---

3. *Qiran-us-Sadain*, p. 169 -70.

Nizamud-din Auliya in the year of accession proved too much and he followed his *pir* to the grave soon after (1325). His long association with the court which lasted from the reign of Kaiqubad till the accession of Muhammad bin Tughlaq is in itself a testimoney of his ability as a courtier who had learnt the art of steering clear with accession of every new Sultan and that too in an age when the accession of new Sultan meant promotion of his own favourits. No wonder then, he got disgusted with the court life and advised his son not to join the court, and waste his whole life in 'spinning yarn' which he had done.

Amir Khusrau was a sufi, a poet, a musician and courtier combined into one. The blending of these qualities into one marks him as a dynamic personality with an irresistible porsonal charm to influence a surrounding in which he would be present. He devoted, a greater part of his time in the court and yet could find time to compose poems, keep the company of the Sufis and yet still could get time to devote himself to the study and practice of music. Amir Khusrau's contribution to music is no mean[4] but he was essentially a literature, and in that field he stands as an outstanding figure of his age. His works testify to his command over the language and his language and his punctilious selection of words speaks volumes for his taste. As a poet Amir Khusrau remained unrivalled. Maulana Jami (1414–1492) a renouned poet of Persia was full of praise for Khusrau's poems. Amir Khusrau was a prolific writer too. According to Firishta he wrote ninety-two books but Maulana Jami puts the number at ninety-nine. arani says that Amir Khusrau composed almost a whole library. But the entire works of Amir Khusrau is not available, though whatever is avaliable by itself is a rare achievement for any individual. The available poetical composition of Amir Khusrau can be grouped into four major categories, poem of adolescence period, poems of middle life, poems of maturity and poems of perfection. Amir Khusrau

4. Barani, p. 359.

was essentially a poet and he should be judged as such. The compositions that contain historical material should be viewed more as source material, as mine of information, and not as histories, written by him a burden which at no stage he claimed for himself. While examining his works as historical source material one will have to bear in mind that he was primarily a poet and a poets reaction to events are not necessarily the same always.

A modern writer[5] has discovered in Amir Khusrau a tension that dominated his life. "The tension which divided Amir Khusrau's loyalty between the esoteric and political Islam, is analogous to another set of tensions in relation to the Indian environment, an irresitible attraction to the life and landscape of India, and an implacable hostility to Hinduism and to the political and military resistance of Hindu India to Muslim rule." However it is doubtful if Amir Khusrau really had some such tension. Throughout his writings we find expressions of his affectionate response to the Indian environment. As a poet and a musician he was imotionally involved and looked at human beings with a different angle, appreciating whatever was good and denouncing the defects. Thus he unhesitatingly condemns rebellious Hindus, but not because they are Hindus but because they are rebellious i.e. he disapproves the rebellious behaviour. One can discern this attitude of Amir Khusrau from narration of the meeting of Kaiqubad with Bughra Khan.

Our main concern for the present is to examine only such works of Amir Khusrau which contain informations useful for reconstructing history. Amir Khusrau, who never claims to be a historian, uses his poetical talents freely in such works, with the result that his narrations are full of exaggerations and metaphorical phraseology. The real importance of his works rests on rich historical information, which with patience and care one can easily discover. While

5. Aziz Ahmad, *Islamic Culture in the Indian Environment*. p. 115.

trying to find evidence in Khusrau's work one may very well keep in mind the surroundings in which he was writing. According to Dr. Ashraf : "Khusrau came from the people and feels at his best only when he moves among the crowd. When behaving as a courtier or as a man of letters, he is conscious of playing a part : his ascetic and puritan moods are decidedly morbid and only temporary, and he avails himself of the first opportunity to throw away these masks and morbid gloom and to start laughing and pleasing himself like other people. Nay, to assure the crowd that no amount of intellectual attainments and secular elevation can stop him from being congenial to them, he even borrows sometimes the vulgarity of the undeveloped mind, and the unrefined taste of the illiterate. When he is among common people he takes a detached view of his previous stately environments and spiritual heights and gives an nonest and frank opinion about men and things, not excluding himself. In trying to express himself with this attitude of mind, however, he finds sometimes that plain and easily intelligible language is not altogether discreet and may involve him in trouble. This shrewdness drives him to subterfuge. He now deliberately takes to grandiloquent style, to florid and bombastic language, and to puns and puzzles ; but he must speak out his mind, as it were, to relieve his agitated and indignant soul. Thus, he takes good care to conceal his meaning in a mass of words, but is still as clear as possible if one knows his feelings and his surroundings .. But if these documents are carefully examined they yield interesting and instructive information of a varied character, besides many graphic descriptions of various social phenomena and references to manners and morals."[6]

HIS WORKS

(i) *Qiran-us-Sadain* was composed in 1289 at the suggestion of Sultan Kaiqubad. The theme of the poem deals with a

6. K. M. Ashraf, *Life and Conditions of the People of Hindustan* (1970) p. 15-16.

single event of history—thc meeting of the father and the son. The meeting was an important event of the early Turkish rule in India. The father was the governor of Bengal whereas the son was the Sultan of Delhi and as such suzerain of the former. In a composition of this type Amir Khusrau had really spun a yarn, but he has incorporated some valuable information. His description of Delhi in detail provides a graphic picture of the capital and its topography and some of its important buildings. He narrates the movement of the royal army towards east to meet the advancing forces of the governor of Bengal. Amir Khusrau presents the picture as though Bughra Khan was marching to occupy Delhi, but concludes by stressing the end when the felial affection prevailed and Bughra Khan trying to impress on his son that his aim in moving towards Delhi was only to meet his son who was then the Sultan. Amir Khusrau also mentions the advice given by Bughra Khan to his son on the manner on conducting state affairs. Though there is nothing unusual in the advice but it hints at the concept of monarchy that had acquired currency among the Turks in India.

(ii) *Miftah-ul-Futuh* was composed by Amir Khusrau in June 1291, and contains the conquest or the victories of Jalalud-din Khalji which were achieved by him during the first year of his reign. It is useful in ascertaining the date of the accession of Jalalud-din Khalji and also throws light on the revolt of Malik Chhajju at Kara and its suppression. The poem also contains an account of Sultan's attempt to conquer Ranthambhor. The poem is not a long one and forms a part of Amir Khusrau's third divan, *Ghurrat-ul-Kamal*. Amir Khusrau gives three reasons for composing this poem. (1) "That I sholud be able to repay for the bounties bestowed by the Sultan upon me." (2) "That nothing remains permanently in this world, perhaps this composition may attain permanency." (3) "That just as the name of the Sultan will be remembered my name will also be remembered, and with the blessings of God I may receive rich reward from the Sulta n."

(iii) *Khazain–ul-Futuh,* completed in 1311 is the only historical composition in prose. Amir Khusrau has used a very high flown metaphorical language. While reading it one feels that Amir Khusrau has deliberately subordinated the narratives to the aesthetic effect which he wanted to create. As the title indicates, it deals with the compaigns and victories of Sultan Alaud-din Khalji. It is extremely important and informative in understanding the Deccan campaign of Malik Kafur, and provides useful information regarding the method adopted in setting up camps and movement of the army and its organisation when on march. For the reign of Alaud-din Khalji, *Khazain-ul-Futuh* is the only contemporary source. "The historical importance of this work," says Dr. K. S. Lal, "can hardly be exaggerated as technically it is the only contemporary history of Alaud-din's reign for even Barani wrote long after the death of the King. Besides the Deccan campaigns which are dealt with exhaustively Khusrau also describes in this work the buildings constructed by Alaud-din, his conquests of Gujarat, Chittor, Malwa and Sevena as well as his administrative measures. From its numerous topographical details, it appears that the author was an aye-witness to at least some of the scenes described in the course of the Deccan compaigns. According to Badaoni, he had accompanied Kafur to the South."[7]

(iv) *Deval Rani Khizr Khan* was composed by Amir Khusrau in 1316, but during the reign of Ghiyasud-din Tughlaq he added some more verses to complete the tragic story of prince Khizr Khan. The core of the story according to Amir Khusrau was supplied to him by the prince personally which he developed in poetical form. This deals primarily with the marriage of Khizr Khan with Deval Rani the daughter of Rai Karan of Gujarat. It supplies superficial information and one may read it more as romantic poem than as history. A literary critic may find more material, but for the purpose of history it hardly supplies any information of value.

7. Dr. K. S. Lal, *History of the Khaljis*, p. 362.

(v) *Nuh Sipihr* is the product of Amir Khusrau's period of poetical perfection. The composition consisting of 4509 verses was finished by Amir Khusrau in 1318 when he was 67 years of age. The work is divided into nine parts. The work was produced at the command of Sultan Mubarak Shah Khalji. Probably Amir Khusrau could not find many qualities in the Sultan to devote his entire work to the praise of the Sultan, thus in first two parts he finishes the conquests and other works of the Sultan, the remaining seven he devotes to describe the country and its flora and fauna for which he seems to have developed an intense fascination. He dialates upon the greatness of Hindustan and even compares it with Khura-san to prove that Hindustan in which he lived was superior. Aziz Ahmad doubts the sincerity of Amir Khusrau and remarks: "Reading these arguments one wonders how far Khusrau is serious. They occur in *Nuh Sipihr* which was a command performance, written for Qutbud-din Mubarak Shah Khalji whose favourite Khusrau Khan was a convert from Hinduism and all powerful at the court. perhaps it was politic and fashionable at that juncture to praise India."[8] But a critical study will surely reveal that these were the outpour of a poet's genuine reactions and feelings. Whatever historical defects one may find in *Nuh Sipihr* one feature of the work will remain undisputed, that it is a mine of information about the country and is extremely informative to construct the social and cultural history of the period. Besides, the action and reaction of the Hindus and the Muslims towards each other in daily life one can find from this work. These informations are not to be found in other contemporary or near contemporary Persian works.

(vi) *Tughlaq Nama* is the last of the historical compositions of Amir Khusrau. It deals with assasination of Qutub-ud-din Mubarak Shah and end of the house of the Khaljis; the rule of Nasirud-din Khusrau Shah; the revolt of Tughlaq Shah and his correspondence with the nobles of the empire, and finally the march of Tughlaq Shah upon Delhi and his victory over

8. Aziz Ahmad, *Loc. cit.*, p. 116.

Khusrau Shah. It was composed sometimes towards the close of 1320. Though it was written at the command of the new Sultan, Ghiyas-ud-din Tughlaq Shah and naturally must contain some praise for him, but it reveals more facts than the much credited *Tarikh-i-Firuz Shahi* of Barani. Amir Khusrau has high lighted the weakness of Qutb-ud-din and the settled government of Khusrau Shah in which all the officers of the army wished to pay allegience to him except Tughlaq Shah. Amir Khusrau had to resort to subterfuge but one can discern that by implication he has pointed out that Tughlaq Shah was a rebel against the established rule of the day.

C. ZIAUDDIN BARANI 1285-1357

Ziaud-din Barani has not mentioned his date of birth anywhere, but towards the end of *Tarikh-i-FiruzShahi* he mentions his age as 74 years[1], and in the preface of the work he mentions that he completed the work in 758/1357,[2] On the basis of this information we may calculate that he was born in 684/1285-6 i.e. during the reign of Balban. He came of a respectable family, and Barani traces his family ties with the Sayyids. His mother came from the Sayyid family of Kaithal and the grandmother of his father Muid-ul Mulk also belonged to the family of Sayyid Jalalud-din of Kaithal. The Sayyid family of Kaithal enjoyed a reputation for their purity of blood and high standard of education and culture, and it seems Barani takes special pride in mentioning this connection to establish the superior blood that ran through his veins.

Muid-ul Mulk served as a *naib* of Arkali Khan during the reign of Jalal-ud-din Khalji, and seems to have been quite prosperous, as Barani mentions that his father had build a large mansion in Kilokheri (Delhi). During the first year of his reign Alaud-din Khalji appointed Muid-ul-Mulk as *Khawaja* and *naib* of Baran (Bulandshahar).[3] Barani's uncle

1. *Tarikh-i-Firuz Shahi*, p. 573.
2. *ibid.*, p. 23.
3. *ibid.*, p. 248.

Alaul-Mulk was one of the trusted friends of Alaud-din Khalji and ended his life as Kotwal of Delhi in the fifth year of his reign.[4]

Ziaud-din Barani had a good education. He finished the study of Quran in the reign of Jalalud-din Khalji. Jalalud-din ascended the throne in 689[5] and was assasinated on Ramazan 17, 695.[6] Thus Barani was five years at the time of the accession of Jalalud-din and about twelve years at the time of his death.

During the reign of Alaud-din Khalji and his successors Barani seems to have lived a comfortable life and did not care for a regular profession or a career. Though he kept the company of scholars and devoted his time to the study of the courses that were available during the age, he led more or less the life of a delinquent. Though younger in age he joined the company of Amir Khusrau and Amir Hasan Sijji and also became a desciple of Shaikh Nizamuddin Aulia. Thus Barani was thirteen years when Alaud-din ascended the throne, and was about thirty-two years at the time of the accession of Qutbud-din Mubarak Shah. During the reign of Muhammad bin Tughlaq he seems to have succeeded in getting state patronage when he was appointed as *nadim* by the Sultan and in that capacity he served the Sultan for seventeen years and three months,[7] the termination being the result of the demise of the Sultan. Barani was then sixty nine years old.

Muhammad bin Tughlaq died in Thatta where Firuz Shah was elected as Sultan, but in Delhi Khwaja-i-Jahan raised another person to the throne. Barani who was then at Delhi must have been implicated in the so-called rebellion of Khwaja-i-Jahan, since the wazir had the concurrence of all

4. *ibid.*, 237.
5. *Miftah-ûl-Futuh,* (Aligarh) p. 7.
6. Barani, p. 230.
7. *ibid.*, p. 504.

persons in the capital and Barani was not the man to go against the general feeling. In the new regime he was looked upon as an associate of the Khwaja-i-Jahan. In the beginning of Firuz Shah's reign Barani was interned in the fort of of Bhatner, and passed his days in anxiety for about five months awaiting the decision of the government. His life was spared, by Firuz Shah as he mentions, "I Zia-i-Barani . .. fell into a variety of mortal dangers. Ill wishers, rivals and enemies strove for my death. I was driven to madness by the polo-sticks of their hatred. They attributed to me a thousand kind of poisonous words before his majesty. If . . . . . . the Sultan of the age, Firuz Shah-us Sultan. had not come to my rescue, and if he had heard and accepted the poisoned words of the powerful and influential enemies of this weak creature, I would have been sleeping in the womb of mother earth."[8]

Barani's life was spared but his property was confiscated and the remaining years of his life he spent in poverty. The abusive phrases with which his works abound indicate that he might have been useing poisonous words to please the late Sultan. Because, after all, Barani presents for himself a mean character who did not even hesitate to use abusive pharaes against Khwaja-i-Jahan just to ingratiate himself with the new regime. However, the period of poverty and privation proved beneficial to the posterity and retained his name for the future. It is during this period that he took to writing, thus at the age of sixty-nine we find an old idler suddenly turned into an author. It was during his internment that Barani became conscious of his past sins and thought that the only means through which he could attain salvation was by writing a life of the Prophet. So in haste he composed the *Sana-i-Muhammadi* or *Nat-i-Muhammadi*. Prof. Habib remarks : "The effort of composing the *Sana-i-Muhammadi* turned Barani who had hitherto been a *diletante* and a young gentleman of leisure, into a professional author. In spite of his old age and poverty, book after book was composed by him in the

8. *ibid.*, p. 557.

next six or seven years. At the age of sixty nine (luner) years he became concious of a profession as well as a mission. Very few authors in world history have begun their life's work so late".[9]

HIS WORKS

Sayyid Mubarak Kirmani generally known as Amir Khurd has mentioned that Barani composed the following books.

(i) *Sana-i-Muhammadi.*

(ii) *Salat-i-Kabir.*

(iii) *Inayat Nama-i Ilahi.*

(iv) *Ma'asir-i Sadat.*

(v) *Tarikh-i Firuz Shahi.*

(vi) *Hasrat Nama.*

It is obvious from the list that Amir Khurd was not aware of all of his works. *Fatawa-i Jahandari* and *Tarikh-i Firuzshahi* which directly concern us, and while using these works we shall have to remember the conditions under which he laboured with no reference works, no resources and no access to office records. He had no means of making sure of a date or a fact. He had to depend entirely on his memory and used his imagination to write his books. Of course, as a clever writer he postulates: "The facts of history are not based on *sanad* (documentory proofs) and evidence." Prof. Habib remarks: "But a non-official historian, like Barani, who records contemporary events and is unable to reach the government archives, has no alternative but to record popularly known facts or what he had learnt from individuals, whose names he may not be in a position to mention."[10]

"It was no credit to the government of Firuz Shah" writes Prof. Habib, "that it had purposely left the great

9. *Medieval India Quarterly*, Vol. III Nos. 3 & 4 p. 201.
10. *ibid.*, p. 205

scholar to die in distress but Amir Khurd had to wield his pen with care and draw a veil over the whole affair. The statement that Barani retired from the service at his own request and that he got a pension from the government of Firuz Shah are both incorrect."[11]

The circumstances in which Barani was writing makes it almost imperative to keep in mind, while reading his *Tarikh-i Firuz Shahi*, the character and mental condition of the author. The agony and the mental torture from which Barani was suffering is reflected throughout his *Tarikh-i Firuz Shahi* and *Fatawai-i Jahandari*.

With a failing memory the old man recounts things of the past when he was very young which create doubt about the varacity of the narratives. For example, when he narrates the pleasures of the reigns of Kaiqubad and Jalalud-din Khalji and pines for them in his old age one is more inclined to take them as an old man's unsatiated desire than evidence of real truth. *Tarikh* is full of such narratives and scholars have used them as evidence for the respective two reigns. Barani's *Tarikh-i Firuz Shahi* has many short comings which are the results of his lapses of memory and resulted in the jumbling up of different events. Historians following him had no suspicion about this and had more than often copied whatever Barani had written in his *Tarikh*. His dates are often inaccurate and very often he avoids giving a date. He hardly follows a chronological sequence but narrate the events in the cause and effect sequence in which they had become fixed in his mind.

At the time of his writing the *Tarikh*, his sufferings were due to the regime of all-powerful Khan-i-Jahan Maqbul and hence on one pretext or the other he spins a yarn to condemn men of low birth. To him converted muslims were of low origin *vis-a-vis* himself a pure Turk. His hatred for the *Hindus* he has ventilated throughout the work. Though he

---

11. *ibid.*, p. 199.

claims to have been a disciple of Shaikh Nizamud-din Aulia and that he had spent his life in the company of the Sufis, he does not indicate any influence of this section on his life or thought. Barani discovered for himself the method of introducing dialogues and conversations of different personalities and through these dialogues he freely ventiletes his own ideas and fellings.

Such dialogues of Barani one may recount under the following heads :

(1) Sultan Balban and his sons Muhammad and Bughra Khan.

(2) Bughra Khan and Sultan Kaiqubad.

(3) Fakhrud-din, the Kotwal of Delhi and his nephew Nizamud-din.

(4) Sultan Jalalud-din and Malik Ahmad Chap.

(5) Sultan Alaud-din and Malik Ala-ul Mulk.

(6) Sultan Alaud-din and Qazi Mughisud-din.

(7) Sultan Muhammad bin Tughlaq and Barani himself.

These diaiogues when compared with his another work *Fatawa-i Jahandari* reveal that they are his own ideas put into the mouths of others. Thus Barani's history *Tarikh-i Firuz Shahi* becomes a very unreliable source. One can neither reject it in the absence of any other source nor accept it in totality, with the result that a modern historian can use his work to interpret in whichever way he likes. The way he turns and twists without care or delibarately neglecting the chronological sequence of events during the reign of Muhammad bin Tughlaq. During his rule he enjoyed the maximum benefit from the Sultan and yet paints him in relation to the events as the chief villain of the drama. A modern historian may discover his impartiality in viewing at events, yet others may discover his power of analysing the causes for the troubles, and in the like manner one may discover them as simple lies to please those who were against

Muhammad bin Tughlaq and were then in power, whom Barani was trying to win over through his *Tarikh*. There can be no end to such speculations which have certainly immortalised Barani as a historian of medieval India.

Of course, modern historographers will discover, Barani's philosophy of history, his treatment, his methology but we have in mind that Barani was an introvert, his conscience was pricked and he attributed his misfortune to his moral failure. So his *Tarikh* was practical, intended to be a double offering ; to God to gain His forgiveness and atone for his sins ; to the Sultan, to secure his patronage and thereby freedom from want and protection from calumny of his enemies.

D. SHAMS SIRAJ AFIF

It is difficult to ascertain the exact date of birth of Shams Siraj Afif, beyond the point except when he says that he was twelve years when Firuz Shah after his return from Thatta brought the two Asokan pillars to his new capital Firozabad (Delhi).[1] Mahdi Husain places the incident in 769/1367, but Rieu, in his catalogue of Persian Manuscript in British Museum places the incident in 763. Thus according to Rieu, Afif was born in 751 and according to Mahdi Husain's reckoning in 757. From the narrations of incidents Mahdi Husain's date seems to be more correet, and we may hypothetically place the year of our author's birth in 757/1356. The ancestors of Afif were very closely associated with the house of Tughlaq Shah, and Firuz Shah. Sadul Mulk Afif, the grate grandfather of Afif, was in the service of Tughlaq Shah and had brought about the marrage of Rajab with Bibi Kadbanu, the daughter of Ranamal Bhatti of Abuhar. Afif mentions that his grandfather Shams Shihab Afif was born on the same day when Firuz Shah was born.[2] He further claims that the ladies of the household of his

1. *Tarikh-i-Firuz Shahi*, p. 310.
2. *ibid*, p. 39

ancesters regularly used to visit *Makhdum-i-Jahan* the mother of Sultan Muhammad bin Tughlaq, and that his great grand-mother used to claim that she had acted as wet nurse to Firuz Shah a fact, which he says, Firuz Shah used to recall to his father and uncle. Afif's father served under Firuz Shah in different capacities ; at one stage he used to take night-muster of the slaves and at another he was attached to the *Diwan-i-Wizarat.*[3] He also accompanied the Sultan in his Nagarkot and Jajnagar expeditions. Afif used to attend the court of Firuz Shah alongwith the officers of *Diwan-i-Wazarat* and subsequently used to join the hunting parties of the Sultan. These instances indicate that Afif had enough opportunities to acquire personal knowledge about the reign and the government of Firuz Shah Tughlaq, and for earlier portions his knowledge could have been easily supplimented by his father, uncle and other relations, all of whom seem to have been in the service of Firuz Shah. Sultan Firuz Shah died on 18th Ramazan 790, September, 20, 1388 when Afif, according to our rackoning, was mature about thirty four lunar years, and enough to understand the entire atmosphere of the reign of Firuz Shah.

Tairikh-i-Firuz-Shahi, the only work of Shams Siraj Afif which has survived seems to be only a part of his bigger work dealing with the history of the Tughlaqs as he himself refers to the *manaqibs* of Sultan Ghiyasud-din Tughlaq Shah, Sultan Muhammad bin Tughlaq Shah and Sultan Muhammad bin Firuz Shah Tughlaq. He also refers to the sack of Delhi by Timur. Thus the part available to us seems to be only a part of the book which he wrote after the destruction of Delhi and the ruin of the Tughlaqs. The title *Tarikh-i-Firuz Shahi* truely speaking have been appended to the surviving portion just for the sake of conveninence and is not the name given by the author. Even the portion available is not the complete history of Firuz Shah, because at one place Afif mentions, "Maulana Ziaud-din Barani in his *Tarikh-i-Firuz*

3. *ibid.*, p. 127, 197.

Shahi has narrated the events from the accession of Sultan Ghiyasud-din Balban upto the end of the sixth year of the reign of Firuz Shah. He had planned to write the history of Firuz Shah in 101 chapters but could write only eleven chapters. Because he could not complete his work the present writer has devoted ninety chapters to it. These ninety chapters have been divided into five parts each parts having eighteen chapters."[4] Of the fifth part only fifteen chapters are available, the rest are lost and we cannot find the end of the reign of Firuz Shah from his work. Thus the entire work of the writer not being available any attempt to find motives of the author to write this history would be at best only hypothetical. Afif seem to have a better idea of writing history and has divided his work in parts relating to one aspect and adding appropriate headings to these parts and the chapters.

Dr. J. M. Banerjee[5] has given a fair assessment of the merit of his work and his remarks are worth nothing, "Afif's style of writlng is interesting Besides details of political events he has described the system of administration, organization of army, various factories, the provision made for maintenance of slaves and for providing employment to the unemployed etc. He refers to the introduction of the practice of striking hours and gives a graphic description as to how some Asokan pillars were removed to there present sites. He does not mince matters while referring to the corrupt practices which developed during the reign of Firuz Shah Tughlaq."

"Afif concludes this historical work with information on the life of the nobles, and perhaps this is his greatest contribution. It brings out clearly the economic contrast amongst various classes of society. Habits of extravagance indulged in by those belonging to higher ranks have been described as also in certain cases the licentiousness of the order of nobility."

4. *ibid.*, p. 30
5. J. M. Banerjee, *History of Firuz Shah Tughlaq* (1967), pp. 207-8

"The work of Afif also throws some light on the llfe of the common people, e. g , the writer mentions that the Sultan strove hard to ameliorate the misery of girls of middle class families by making suitable provision for their dowries . . . . . Afif is also coloured by religious prejudices. He has painted the Sultan as an ideal Muslim whose actions streamed from religious motive. Even in his account of *Tas-i-Ghariyal* the writer fails to apreciate its general utility to all, and only insists upon its religious utility to the Muslims. Throughout his narrative he has praised the Sultan, and concealed the latter's weakness under one cloak or another, e.g., the Sultan's lack of military skill has been justified on the ground of his idealism. The writer's appreciation of the Sultan's generosity and kindness illustrated with the narration of the various an cdotes of his life, incedentally exposes the administrative inefficiency and the corruptions of the age."

The manner in which Afif mentions the weakness of the character of Firuz Shah and tries to cover it up under the garb of one or other explaination ; narrates the weakness that had crept into the administration ; often makes one wonder, whether he was writing his *manaqib* actually in appreciation of Firuz Shah or was trying to criticise him by painting his as a religious person who in the name of religion was actually bringing about the ruin of the Tughlaq dynasty and was sapping the administration of its vital force. While granting all sorts of lattitude to the nobility, as Afif states, Firuz Shah managed to have a smooth sailing for himself. He left a tottering kingdom which crumbled down with the attack of Timur, the symptoms of which were visible during his last days. The answer to these doubts, however, cannot be stated with absolute certainty. It is also difficult to accept that Afif was advocating the causes that brought about the ruin of the ruling class to which he belonged. During the medieval times the conception of class and persons thinking in terms of class did not exist. Every individual lived for himself and thought for himself. Thus one feels more inclined to think with Peter Hardy that "for Afif there is no organic relation between the biography of Firuz Shah Tughlaq and the history of his time. History exists only to reveal what existed before history—that is, Firuz Shah Tughlaq's divinely created perfect nature. History, that is events, does not itself mould and develop the sultan's characteristics, it merely provides a stage for their manifestation. It was known and foretold almost as soon as the sultan was born that he was destined to be the man of his age. Nor does Firuz Shah, the human being, through his acts influence the history of his time. The realm is prosperous, prices are low, the Sultan, receives recognition from the caliph not because he acts, but because he exists. The presence of a saint in north India and a regime of peace and prosperity are connate concomitants, not historical causes and effects. For Afif, these phenomena are merely complementary aspects of the great, divinely ordained, order of Being."[6]

E. ALI BIN MAHMUD AL KIRMANI

and

MA'ASIR-I-MAHMUDSHAHI

Ma'asir-i-Mahmudshahi is one of the Provincial histories written in the kingdom of Malwa during the fifteenth century and the purpose to inculde it is to indicate the change that had come into the writing of history by the fifteenth century. It is generally held that with the coming of the Mughals official histories of the empire written by royal historiographers was started in India and that Abul Fazl was the first such historian. An examination of the contents of *Ma'asir-i-Mahmudshahi* however, reveals that the process had started earlier.

Ma'asir-i-Mahmudshahi is a contemporary history of Sultan Mahmud Khalji I of Malwa who ruled from 1436 to 1469. The author mentions the name of the history as : This history accepted the name of *Ma'asir-i-Mahmudshahi wa Siyar-i-Khilafat-panahi* "The author mentions his name in the following words :

6. P. Hardy, *Historians of Medieval India*, (London 1960) p. 51.

"The compilor of these chronicles and the narrator of these merits, the servant of God the Affectionate, hoping His mercy is Ali bin Mahmud al Kirmani known as Shihab Hakim." We have very little information about the anticidents of Shihab Hakim but from the stray references scattered in the text we may deduce that he belonged to the class of fresh immigrants from Persia (Kirman) and had settled down in the kingdom of Jaunpur where he had established his reputation as a scholar before coming to Malwa. It seems that Mahmud Khalji was keen on getting an official history written by some competent writer and had deputed persons in search of such a scholar. Shihab Hakim seems to have come to know of it and was keen on getting the assignment. He left Jaunpur sometime in 1465 and came to Ranthambhor from where he left for Shadiabad (Mandu), but on reaching Shadiabad he learnt that the Sultan was encamped at Azizabad and without waiting he immediately proceeded to that place. He had his first opportunity of meeting the Sultan at Azizabad in 1465. Sultan Mahmud received him well and allowed him to attend court, but some prominent persons created suspicion about him in the mind of the Sultan who became indifferent towards him. Shihab Hakim, however, remained in the camp of the Sultan and returned with his entourage when the Sultan returned to Shadiabad. At Shadiabad he picked up friendship of Shaikh Alaud-daula at whose residence he met Prince Muhammad known as Ghiyas Shah. He impressed the Prince with his compositions and the Prince recommended him to the Sultan and also presented some of his compositions for royal inspection. He also dispelled the doubts and suspicions that had been created by others.

Sultan Mahmud Khalji who wanted that a history of his reign should be written appreciated the scholarship of Shihab Hakim and on the recommendation of Prince Ghiyas Shah entrusted the work to him. From a reading of the text we find it clearly stated that *Ma'asir-i-Mahmudshahi* was an outcome of Sultan Mahmud's desire to compile a history of his reign and that the task was entrusted to Shihab Hakim by Sultan Mahmud himself. The author writes : "It was indicated by the king to complete the records of his sublimilities and glories which was a good news for me; and the words from his tongue that our (his) history depended on the coming of the beggar that is myself" Sachau and Ethe have concluded that the book was written "after the king's death at the command of his son and successor Sultan Ghiyas-al-duniya wa-al-din Muhammad." A full reading of the text, however, points out the error of the cataloguers. The text yields the following points.

1. We find that Sultan Mahmud Shah himself entrusted the work of writing the history of his reign.

2. Throughout the work Sultan Mahmud Khalji had been addressed as a living King. "The auspicious sitting of the king on the throne of the kingdom which may last till the day of resurrection."

3. The work was completed in one year's time. "In a year this treasure weighing mind brought out the treasures from the ocean of heart."

4. Towards the end of the book Shihab Hakim wishes Noah's age for Sultan Mahmud which implies that he was alive. "This history of the civil and military rules of the time and the world...whose age may equal the age of Noah."

5. After completion of the book Shihab Hakim speaks of presenting the book before Sultan Mahmud. "The aim of the manifestation of these virgin bridges, who have come out of their bridal chamber of thought, after getting polished and decorated (was that they) may get the audience of the king (who was) of the perfect mind, comprehensive opinion, brightness and sagacity of the Mercury. the wisdom of Alexander and Plato, the diver of the ocean of thoughts and jeweller of the market of subtlities of rheotoric, so that they may get the auspicious approval of the king."

6. From the internal evidence we find that the narratives end in the year 872/1467-8, and that it speaks nothing about the death of Sultam Mahmud, which if the book had been written during the reign of Ghiyas Shah, certainly would have been mentioned.

7. Besides all these arguments, Shihab Hakim has given the date of completion in a chronogram , "If you are seeking for the sign of the date of this history, count from beginning to end '*The faith of the king having the stirup of Heaven.*" In the chronogram the letters according the to *Abjad* calculation yield 872. Thus taking all the evidences we find that the book was completed about a year before the death of Sultan Mahmud

The author of Ma'asir-i-Mahmudshahi was not an eye witness to most of the events he narrates in his work, but he did not write from mere heresay of gossips circulating in the bazars. He was provided with the source material which consisted of different types of documents and certificates etc. Shihab Hakim says that Mahmud Khalji himself ordered for the collection of all such papers which were to be used for the compilation of the history of his reign. "Different folios which were written previously and which were lying with different persons were all collected." The missing portions of events in these parts were compiled afresh on the evidence of such persons who had been present during those events. "And what ever was left was enquired from those people who were present at the time of their happening and who had witnessed the state of affairs with their own eyes". After the collection of all the papers these were put into order and then placed before the Sultan for his inspection and final corrections. "Story by story and event by event after correcting more than once were presented to the king who was pleased to study them. What convinced his fragrant mind and no doubts were left about their authenticity, veracity and freedom from blemish, was indicted to be written".

The Sultan on inspection did make final corrections wherever he found ambiguity or contradiction and for these corrections he consulted trustworthy persons. "If any ambiguity or doubt remained on any event, authenticity was given after enquiring from trusted persons and men in the know and on whose words reliance could be placed for that affair. As all the necessary material was provided by the Sultan, Shihab Hakim does not claim for himself the authorship, on the contrary, he speak of himself only as the compiler. "Therefore the compilation and the arrangement of this history and the narrations of every story, even in its place, is absolutely the result of the generous nature and the brilliant mind of the king. After the different commemorations were collected and corrected, they were entrusted to this slave that is myself according to the Royal orders, obeyed throughout the word." Thus we find that *Ma'asir-i-Mahmudshahi* had for its source material all necessary state-papers records and other papers which bore the stamp of the Sultan and it is therefore, in a way, an official history of the region of Mahmud Shah Khalji. It indicates that writing of history based on the papers which were approved by the ruler had already started in India. This history was compiled by a scholar not in the expectation of reward, but by one who was in the pay of the Sultan for this purpose and had to get approval of the Sultan for every statement made in it. The presentation of history in this form naturally had its defects. It had to reflect the bias and outlook of the ruler, his court, and the social and the religious views expressed in his kingdom. The entire narrative had to move round the king as its centre. May be as a result of the conditions under which Shihab Hakim was writing that in spite of his professing that history should be correct and faithful narrative of events, at many places he overlooks the failure of Mahmud Khalji in some of his military campaigns. He is also not free from his personal prejudices and seems to have an embittered feeling towards the scholars of Malwa, In his entire work he does not supply us with the names of scholars and their achievements except the name of Shaikh Alauddaula at whose residence he met Prince Ghiyas Shah. He also seems to have been weak at numerals and had carefully avoided giving figures of the army and similarly measurements of buildings ; and thus, instead of being definite he remains contended at many places with mere pompous display of language over which he certainly displays a rare command.

Yet with all its defects *Ma'asir-i-Mahmudshahi* is a mine information which is not only important for the history of Malwa but also helpful in understanding the contemporary atmosphere of the fifteenth century India. The extensive account of the marriage of Prince Ghiyas Shah is full of such information that helps in constructing the economic conditions of the time. Shihab Hakim also displays that the earlier idiom of the Sultanate period had not been completely shed off at the time when he was writing. Like earlier chroniclers he too talks of the usefulness of history almost in the same vein. True history according to Shihab Hakim should be correct and faithful narrative of events. History for him was not meant for ordinary men. It was like a guide-book for the kings who could learn many lessons from the results of the past. The stories of generosity, justice, good administration and conquests of various countries of the past kings tell how these virtues bring their reward. It also tells what catastrophies fall as a result of misdeeds, mal-administration, cruelty and foolish acts. These narratives pre-warn the readers about the results of their actions. The 'readers' here are meant to be rulers and administrators and not any reader. The wise, says he, therefore, get warnad and are thereby prevented from taking wrong steps.

9

Abul Fazl's Conception of Monarchy

Abul Fazl, while writing the history of Akbar, it seems, felt the need of giving justification to the actions of his monarch. That Akbar was an ideal monarch could be established by setting down standards for the institution of monarchy which would well square with his actions. Though the institution of monarchy had entered into Islamic civilisation long before Abul Fazl and other Muslim theologians came forward with their justifications for the institution, yet the idea that sovereignty essentially belonged to Allah and that the rulers were no more than His servants on earth, had persisted in the Islamic conception. Abul Fazl in his conception of monarchy, however, tried to give a fresh interpretation.

Abul Fazl started his discussion with the need on the cause of existance of a monarch. He pre-supposed the evil nature of man which tends to corrupt as a result of his greed, selfishness and lust, and to keep them in order, according to him, monarch is a necessity. According to Abul Fazl, "If royalty did not exist, the storm of strife would never subside, nor selfish ambitions disappear. Mankind, being under the burden of lawlessness and lust, would sink into the pit of distruction ; the world, this great market place, would lose its prosperity, and the whole earth become a barren waste. Royalty is a remedy for these. A king is the origin of stability and possession."[1]

Here Abul Fazl is obviously drawing upon *Mahabharata* for his interpretation. *In Mahabharata* the warrior-sage Bhisma traces the origin of kingship to the absence of order among the mankind in the remote past.[2] The people being without a king, points out the sage, met with destruction by devouring one another, like the stronger fish devouring the

---

1. *Ain-i-Akbari*, (henceforth simply *Ain.*) Tr., Vol. I, p. 2
2. *Shantiparva*, XII, 67.

weaker ones in water. The people gathered together and tried to stop the abuses by mutual agreement which having failed they collectively waited on Brahma, the creator, and prayed for a lord who would protect them and whom they would honour collectively. Thus came the king into being who restored order by striking terror into the hearts of the evil doers and forcing the people to follow the *dharma*. Thus Abul Fazl's statement, that Royalty is a remidy and that a king is origin of stability and possession, is almost identical with that of the *Mahabharata*.

The ruler in Islam was not the peoples master but only held in trust for the Supreme Being. Abul Fazl, however, considers his monarch as divine. According to him "Royalty is a light emanating from God, and a ray from the Sun, the illuminator of the universe, the argument of the book of perfection, the receptacle of all virtues.[3] It is communicated by God to kings without the intermediate assistance of anyone. At another place Abul Fazl says "Kingship is a gift not bestowed till many thousand good qualities have been gathered together in an individual."[4] The extent to which Abul Fazl's ideas are in confirmity with Indian mythology can be seen from the following instance given in detail in the *Mahabharata*. According to the story, it was in the time of Prithu, the seventh in the generation of the line of rulers,[5] that true

3. *Ain*. I, (tr.) p. 3.
4. *Akbar Nama*, II (tr.) p. 285.
5. According to the mythological story, the first was Virajas the mind-begotten son of the Great God. He and his son and grandson were ascetics and thus could not carry out the work. The fourth and the fifth were good but the former was deficient in *dandamit* and the latter was self-indulgent, the sixth called Vena was swayed by passions of anger and hatred and was unrighteous towards his subjects. Vena was killed by the sages who churned his right arm out of which came out Prithu, the seventh ruler in the line.

kingship came into existance. The Divine sanction was set upon Prithu when Vishnu Himself fixed the king's status so that no one else could sure pass him, and still more when He entered the king's person by means of His ascetic power.[6]

Thus, like Prithu Abul Fazl's monarch also gets the Divine elements directly out of which naturally came his authority over the subjects. Monarchy being a light emanating from God and communicated by him directly, has many inherent qualities which automatically enter into the possessor of this light. According to Abul Fazl, a monarch, because of the Divine light in him, possesses besides others, the following qualities.

1. A paternal love towards his subjects :

Thousands find rest in the love of the king : and sectarian differences do not rise the dust of strife. In his wisdom the king will understand the spirit of the age and shape his plans accordingly

2. A large heart :

The sight of anything disagreeable does not upset him. His divine firmness gives him the power of requital, nor does the high position of an offender interfere with it. The wishes of the great and small are attended to and their claims met with no delay at his hands. Akbar himself is said to have expressed that "We by virtue of our being the shadow of God, receive little and give much. Our forgiveness has no relish for vengeance."[7]

3. Daily increasing trust in God :

When he performs an action, he considers God as the real doer of it, so that a conflict of motives can produce no disturbance.

---

6. U. N. Ghoshal, *Indian Political Ideas*, (1966), p. 195.
7. *Akbar Nama*, III (tr.) p. 136.

4. Prayer and devotian :

The success of his plans will not lead him to neglect ; nor will adversity cause him forget God and madly trust in man.

Abul Fazl was writing at a period when Akbar had come to the realisation that in India, a monarch if he is to be successful must recognise all his subjects as equal and all preference for religion and race should disappear in his kingdom. To Abul Fazl such a stand presented a problem. On the one hand he could not paint Akbar as one who had deviated from the True Path, on the other his ideal monarch was not to be bound by limits fixed by any religion. Abul Fazl, therefore, considered it necessary to explain the entire situation by theorising that : Besides being courageous just, benevolent and forgiving, the king must be above religious differences. They must not withhold him from his duty towards all classes of men. All must have repose under him, so that the shadow of God may confer glory. He must possess an ever increasing love towards all his subjects and must bring choice deliberation to bear upon his work and do what is proper for the time. He must possess a hatred for blind following of authority (*taqlid*). Let the love of enquiry always precede and reason (*dalil parasti*) be his guide.[8] Thus, the limits of the boundaries set forth by Islam are pushed further, and the monarch being liberated from the religious limitations the scope of his activitities is widened. Abul Fazl laid down that "in spite of these qualities the king cannot be fit for this lofty office if he does not inaugurate universal peace (*sulah-i-kul*). If he does not regard all conditions of humanity and all sects of religion with the single eye. He should not be mother to some and be step-mother to others or else he will not become fit for the exalted dignity."[9] In Abul Fazl's theory the king was the ruler of mankind, the supreme head of a state in which all religions were to be treated with

8. *Ibid.*, III, (tr.) p. 680.
9. *Ibid.*, II, (tr.) p. 421.

equality. "The sections of mankind who are a divine deposit and treasure must be regarded with the glance of affection. It must be considered that divine mercy attaches itself to every form of creed . . . The Eternal God is bounteous to all souls. Hence it is fitting that kings, who are shadow of divinity, should not cast away the principle" of peace with all.[10]

Prior to Abul Fazl, the authors of works on Islamic polity[11] tried to explain the position and functions of a monarch in a Muslim Kingdom. The divine fiction had also entered in those expositions but with marked narraw sectarian bias, which certainly was contrary to Abul Fazl's ideal. Thus by the time Abul Fazl was writing, the institution of monarchy was fairly old, and himself being a student of history he was fully conscious of the abuse of monarchical powers by so many kings in the past. To distinguish his his ideal king from others, he used the term "true king" for his ideal and "selfish rulers" for others. This distinction, according to Abul Fazl, was due to the fact that all kings were not recipients of "Divine Light", and not being recipients of this grace they could not be true kings. But, according to Abul Fazl, "silly and short-sighted men cannot distinguish a true king from a selfish ruler," and this was so because "both have in common a large treasury, numerous army, clever servants, obedient subjects, an abundance of wise men, a multitude of skilful workmen and a superfluity of means of enjoyment . . . However, men with insight

10. *ibid.*, III. Text, 659 ; Ibn Hasan, p. 62.
11. For example in the *Siyasat Namah* of Nizam ul Mulk Tusi and the *Fatawa-i-Jahandari* of Ziaud din Barani, kingship has been placed on divine pedastal. Both these authors have reoriented the Sasanid ideals with Islamic colouring. They, however conceived the state as consisting of Believers alone, hence by implication their king was to look after the interest of the Believers, the non-believers in such a scheme could have no place.

always discern the difference. In the case of the former, the things ennumerated are lasting, but in that of latter, of short duration."[12]

The object of the true king is to remove oppression and to provide for every thing which is good and therefore, he does not attach himself to the material things that are concomitant of monarchy. He uses them, but only as means and not as an end. As a result of this attitude of the True King, security, health, chastity, justice, polite manners, faithfulness and truth pervade the social order. The selfish ruler, on the other hand is kept in bonds by the external forms of royal power, by vanity, the slavishness of men and the desire of enjoyment ; hence everywhere there is insecurity, disturbance, strife, opposition, treachery and robbery.[13] Thus we find Abul Fazl wanted to say that the complexion of the age depended on the nature of the monarch i.e. the character of society assumed the shape according to as the king happened to be a True King or a False King. The dictum that the king is the cause of the complexion of his age, 'Raja Kalasya karanam" had been current in Indian Political thought from the Mahabharata age.[14] It was believed 'that on the king rests the responsibility for good or bad government, through which according to ancient belief, the complexion of the Yuga (period) in which he lives will be changed for better or worse." The author of *Sukranitisara* also introduced the same idea in the phrase "Yugapravartako raja."[15] Though it would be rather a hasty generalisation to assert that Abul Fazl has borrowed the idea from the *Mahabharata*, but the similarity in the ideas does suggest the direction from where he was drawing his inspiration.

After having stressed the idea that the complexion of the age depends on the king. Abul Fazl proceeded to explain

12. *Ain.* (tr.) I, p. 2.
13. *ibid* , p. 3.
14. Rangaswami Aiyangar, K.V., *Rajadharma*, p. 102.
15. *Sukranitisara*, IV, i, 11, 90-125 (Tr.) B. K. Sarkar.

the method by which the king could achieve this object. According to him the desired aim could be achieved by the king by proper understanding of five types of human character, judicious selection of the four-fold division of state servants and by maintaining a proper balance in the organisation of the four-fold constituents of the political body.[16]

Five Types of Human Character

Abul Fazl describes the types of human character as follows "The most commendable person is *the Sagacious man* who prudently does that which is proper and absolutely necessary. The fountain of his virtues does not only run along his channel but render verdant the fields of other men. Such a one is the fittest person for a king to consult in State affairs. After him comes *the man of good intentions*. The river of his virtues does not flow over its bed, and does not therefore become an irrigating source for others. Although it may be proper to show him kindness and respect, yet he does not merit so high a degree of confidence. Inferior to him is *the simple man*, who does not wear the badge of excellence upon the sleeve of his action, yet keeps the hem of his garment free from the dust of wicked deeds. He does not deserve any distinction ; but ought to be allowed to live at his ease. Worse than him is *the inconsiderate man*, who fills his house with furniture for his own mischief, without, however, doing harm to others. Him the king should keep in the hot place of disappointment, and bring him to the road of virtue by good advice and severe reprehension. The last of all is *the vicious man*, whose black deeds alarm others and throw, on account

---

16. *Ain.* (Tr.) I, p. 4. Abul Fazl says "In the same manner that equilibrium of animal constitution depends upon an equal mixture of elements, so also does the political constitution becomes well tempered by proper division of rank ; and by means of the warmth of the ray of unanimity and concord, a multitude of people become fused into one body."

of their viciousness, a whole world into grief. If the remidies employed in the case of men of the preceding class do not among him the king should consider him a leper, and confine him seperately from mankind : and provided this harsh treatment does not awaken him from his sleep of error, he should feel the torture of grief, and be banished from his dwelling ; and if this remidy produce no effect either, he should be driven out of the kingdom to wander in the wilderness of disappointment ; and if even this should not improve his vicious nature, he should be deprived of the instruments of his wickedness, and lose his sight, or his hand, or his foot. But the king ought not to go so far as to cut the thread of his existence ; for sages consider the human form as an edifice made by God, and do not permit its distruction."[17]

According to Abul Fazl a True King must first of all make himself acquainted with the character of men by his insight and penetration and then regulate the business accordingly,[18] because it was on the proper distribution of the four fold division of state servants based on their character that the successful working of the body politic depended, and so did royalty receive its final tint from it.

The Four-fold Division of State Servants

The nobles of the state, who in reliance on their position lead every thing to a happy issue. Illuminating the battle-field with the halo of devotedness, they make no account of their lives. These fortunate courtiers resemble *fire,* being ardent in devotion and consuming in dealing with foes.

The assistants of victory were the collectors of revenue and those entrusted with income and expenditure, who, in the administration resemble *wind,* at times a heart rejoicing breeze, at other times a hot pestilential blast.

---

17. *ibid.*, p. 8 Blochmann in the foot-note points out that "It is a free paraphrase of a passage in the *Akhlaq-i-Muhsini,* Chapter XXXII entitled *dar Siyasat.*
18. *ibid.*, p. 8.

The companions of the king, who are ornaments of the court by the light of their wisdom, the ray of their sharpsightedness their knowledge of the times, their intimate acquaintance with human nature, their frankness and polite address. Through the excellence of their religious faith and good-will thousands open in the market place of the world the stores of virtue. Wisely fettering ambition of the battle field of the world, they extinguish the spark of wrath by the rain of their wisdom ; whence they resemble *water,* in the affairs of political body. When they are of mild temperament, they remove the dust of affliction from the hearts of men ; but if they depart from moderation, they inundate the world with a deluge of calamity.

The servants, who at court perform the duties about the king. They occupy, in the system of state, the position of *earth.* As such they lie on the high road of submissson and in dust before the majesty of the king. If free from chaff and dross, they are like an elixir for the body, otherwise they are dust and dirt upon the face of success.[19]

The Four-fold Constituent of the Political Body :

Abul Fazl divided the people of the state into four categories on the basis of their professions. The first he called warriors, who in the political body have the nature of *fire.* Their flame directed by understanding, consume the straw and rubbish of rebellion and strife and kindle the lamp of rest in this world of disturbance. The second category consisted of artificers and merchants who hold the place of *air.* Through their labours and travels God's gifts become universal, and the breeze of contentment nourishes the rose tree of life. The third group consisted of the learned such as the philosopher, the physician, the arithmatician, the geometrician and the astronomer, who hold the place of *water.* From their pen and their wisdom a river flows in the draught of the world, and the garden of the universe receives from their

19. *ibid.*, pp. 4-7.

irrigating powers a peculiar freshness. The fourth class was of husbandmen and labourers who may be compared to *earth*. By their efforts the staple of life is brought to perfection, and strength and happiness flow from their work.[20]

The above observation of Abul Fazl indicates that to him the state was like an organic body and like the organic body it is also composed of four elements all of which were equally important for the maintenance of the body. By this comparison he successfully brings out the equality of all the professions because all the four elements were necessary and none of the three could exist in the absence of the fourth. It was in the harmonious blending of these elements that the health of the state could be maintained. This four-fold division of the body political, according to him could be maintained in proper balance by the monarch alone for he says "It is obligatory for a king to put each of these in its proper place, and by uniting personal ability with due respect for others, to cause the world to flourish"[21]

Abul Fazl considered Akbar as his ideal monarch in whom he discovered all the roquisites of a just and true king which according to him, was sufficient proof of the divine origin of his monarch. "Praise be to God," writes Abul Fazl, "The exalted monarch of our time is so endowed with these laudable dispositions, that it is no exaggeration to call him their exordium. From the light of his wisdom, he discerns the worth of men, and kindles the lamp of their energy ; whilst ever clear to himself, and without an effort, he adorns his wisdom with the beauty of practice."[22]

By granting him complete authority over every section and type of people and by tracing divine attributes, Abul Fazl certainly made his monarch a despot. But such a thing as undiluted autocracy could not have existed. Being conscious

20. *ibid.*, p. 4.
21, *ibid.*, p. 4.
22. *ibid.*, p. 9.

of this fact, he laid great stress on the recognition of the spirit of the age by the kiug. At one place he said, "In his wisdom the king will understand the sprit of the age and shape his plans accordingly." Besides, Abul Fazl never intended his ideal monarch to be sectarian in his views and in general conduct of the state business. He said that in spite of all the requisite qnalities the king could not be fit for the lofty office if he did not inaugurate universal peace, and did not treat all conditions of humanity and all sects of religion with singe eye of favour, and "not be mother to one and be step-mother to others."[23]

Limited kingship was something beyond the conception of Abul Fazl, for he argued that all were not competent to give advice or even to participate in deliberations. Being a shadow of God the king received light directly from him. He feared Him alone and trusted Him alone. On earth the king was supreme in his sphere, His power as a ruler was absolute and indivisible. because according to Abul Fazl, "ascetice and sages and politicians who have regard to the repose of mortals regarded that repose bound up with one ruler, one rule one guide, one aim and one thought.[24]

Was Abul Fazl's Conception Anti-Islamic

It is a well known fact that Hindu writers, chief among among them being Manu, attributed divinity to the king. The early Muslims could never have thought of acknowledging divine element in any man. In theory even the Khalifa existed by virtue of the will ol the Muslims people. But aceording to Abul Fazl, the monarch enjoyed his position because of divine will. Hence the greatness and the right to rule was inherent in a monarch. Thus Abul Fazl's theory was autocratic whereas Islamic theory conceived of democracy. The object of the Khalifa was to propogate the gospel of the Prophet Muhammad, but Abul Fazl's monarch was to main-

23. *Akbar Nama*, II (Tr.) p. 421.
24. *ibid.*, III, (Tr.), p. 6.

tain goodwill, concord and peace among the different religions and creeds that existed in his dominions. The Khalifa was to maintain the eternal difference between the Muslims and the non-Muslims but Abul Fazl's Monarch was to place them on the same footing not be mother to one and be step-mother to the other. Abul Fazl's monarch was the head of a political body and not merely a leader of an active and conscious missionary political society. Apparently these differences may look like anti-Islamic, but truely speaking they were not. Islam as preached by the Prophet was not as conservative, sectarian and narrow in its out look as it was later interpreted by the Ulama and the jurists who had their own axe to grind through these interpretations. Abul Fazl spoke of "hatred of sequacity (*taqlid*) as one of the essentials of monarchy. "Let the love of inquiry always precede his actions, and the cult of proof be his method so that he may not be moved from his course by perceiving the view of a multitude, and may not by altercation be made impatient of research." Such a statement of Abul Fazl led Ibn Hasan and Tripathi to conclude that Abul Fazl's monarch was above the religious law. "Thus Abul Fazl's monorch," says Ibn Hasan, "should take no notice of religious. He should act as time demands. He must follow inquiry and not be led by authority. Thus both Islamic law and Hadis cease to be the code of his government,"[25]

Similarly, Dr Tripathi says, "In place of the religious law of the Muslims, Abul Fazl puts the divine will which manifests itself in the institutions of the King. The one believes in the law as laid down by the Quran and the Hadis and other sources, the other puts its faith in the law of God as a true sovereign understands it."[26]

However, with due deference to these two learned scholars one may point out that Akbar never acted in direct contradiction of any injunction laid down in Quranic Law. The

25. Ibn Hasan, *Central Structure of the Mughal Empire*, p. 61.
26. R. P. Tripathi, *Some Aspects of Muslim Administration*, p. 138.

declaration of the Mehzar did not give an authority which was superior to the Quran and Hadis. What Abul Fazl actually aimed at was that the monarch should not allow himself to be dominated by the Ulama who professed to exercise authority. Truely speaking, Abul Fazl had understood the true spirit of the Islamic law and religion and was opposed to those things which were being practised in the name of religion. So far the divine element is concerned, it had entered into Islam long before Abul Fazl came with his theory. During the later Abbasids, when the temporal power of the Khalifa had declined, they tried to compensate for the loss in the temporal power by assuming high sounding religious titles. In those days of decadence the Khalifa was called the 'Viceger rent of God' and the 'Shadow of God on Earth', etc. Since then it became a fashion to apply the above epithets to powerful kings and emperors. Thus, in Abul Fazl's theory, there was hardly anything offensive to the Muslims in general except of course to a few orthodox Sunni Ulama. Strictly speaking in Abul Fazl's concept of sovereignty, the three streams, the Mughal, the Muslim and the Hindu, had mingled into single channel.

10

Religious Policy of Aurangzeb

The religious policy of Aurangzeb is one of the most controversial topics in the history of Medieval India. Scholars who defend Aurangzeb, argue that the measures taken by him were not fanatical but so depicted by different writers are mere exaggerations. In defence of their argument they quote the increase in the number of Hindus in the state employment during his reign and the stray instances of his donation to some Hindu establishment in his vast empire. The present attempt simply aims at findling out whether the policy adopted by him was an outcome of the circumstances in which he ascended the throne, and the situations he was called upon to handle, or it was an outcome of his personal approach to Islam.

To understand the situation one will have to examine the trends and the strands that had come into being in the Mughal Empire from the time of Akbar, who definitely fol'owed a liberal policy—atleast from 1580 onwards— making the state broad-based in which the religious discrimination was not allowed to guide the policy of the state. But with all his eflorts Akbar did not succeed in infusing liberal attitude in the entire Muslim community. It was only the strong hand of the Emperor that kept the fanatical orthodox section subdued, but he could not prevent their mental farmentation which continued unabated below the surface. Thus during the reign of Jahangir while the institutions of Akbar proved too strong to be demolished all atonce or completely suppressed, the group of orthodox element began to show its reactions. The traditions set up by Akbar and the training imparted to Jahangir dominated his personality too much, but his own conscience seems to have been disturbed by the dictates of Islamic religion and the liberalism of Akbar. He could not set aside the liberal traditions of Akbar, but satisfied his conscience by taking sporadic actions in the name of True Faith.[1] The only plansible explanation for such actions seems to be that they gave some satisfation to the Emperor who might have been undergoing a sort of mental discomfort for not strictly observing the tenets of Islam. Of course, Jahangir was not made of stuff to be able to observe strictly the tenets of Islam even if he wanted to do so But the ostensible result of Jahangir's actions was an encouragement to the orthodox element in the Empire. The appearance of Baqi Billah and Shaikh Ahmad Sarhindi, *Majaddid Alf-i-Sani* definitely indicate the re-emergence of the orthodox Muslim revivalist trend in the Muslim society of the Mughal Empire.

1. The examples are not many—
   (i) Punishment of Kaukab, Sharif and Abdul Latif "for the purpose of carrying out the Divine Law in order that the ignorant persons might not be disposed towards the same action." *Tuzuk.* (R. & B.) I p. 171, 5th R. Y. :
   (ii) Ruz-afzun, son of Raja Sangram of Bihar on conversion to Islam "was made Raja of the province of his father." *ibid*, p. 296, 10th R. Y.
   (iii) The destruction of the temple of Varah Avatar at Ajmer and breaking the idol of the temple. *ibid.*, p. 254, 8th R. Y.
   (iv) At Rajauri, Jahangir writes "They (Muslims) ally themselves with Hindus, and both give and take girls. Taking them is good, but giving them, God forbid. I gave an order that hereafter they should not do such thing and whoever was guilty of them, should be capitally punished." *ibid.*, ii, p. 181. 15th R. Y.
   (v) In the sixteenth year of his reign after the conquest of Kangra, Jahangir went to see the fort and "gave an order that the *qazi*, the *Mir Adl*, and other learnded men of Islam should accompany me and carry out in the fort whatever was customary, according

(*Contd. on page* 203)

With the accession of Shahjahan the orthodox section received greater encouragement, because in the outlook of the Emperor they could see a definite leaning towards orthodoxy According to Abdul Hamid Lahori, Shahjahan after his accession abolished the court ettiquete of *sijda*[2] and subsequently in 1636-7 abolished *zaminbos*[3] and introduced instead of these two a new from known as *cuhahartaslim*. The introduction of new form of salutation in itself is not so significant but the abolition of *sijda* and *zaminbos* on the plea that they violated the Islamic injuction is the matter that concerns us. His tendency towards Islamic characteristic of the state became more pronounced by his greater stress on Muslim festivals. Shahjahan reverted back to the practice of desecrating the religious shrines of the rebel chiefs and prohibited the repair of old temples and the construction of new ones.[4] He also ordered for demolition of temples at quite a number of places[5] and some of them were converted into mosques.[6] It is difficult to associate or to find out any particular motive behind these actions of Shahjahan, except that he was trying to satisfy his conscience and was behaving in a manner in which a true Muslim would behave. The effect of these steps, however,

---

(*Contd. from page* 202)

to the religion of Muhammad. Briefly, having traversed about one *koss*, I went up to the top of the fort, and by the grace of God, the call of prayer and the reading of the *khutba* and the slaughter of a bullock, which had not taken place from the commencement of the building of the fort till now, were carried out it my presence." *ibid*., ii, p. 223.

2. *Badshah Nama*, i, p. 110.
3. *ibid.*, p. 112.
4. *ibid.*, p. 452.
5. *ibid.*
6. *ibid*., ii, p. 58 (The temple of Ichchabal was destroyed and converted into a mosque).

on the outlook of the orthodox section of Muslim population was of great importance. In this policy they found a positive encouragement to religious fanaticism and began to feel the return of their domination, the loss of which they were feeling miserably from the time of Akbar. Naturally Shahjahan is painted in their histories as a champion of Islam, although he did not permit the orthodox ulama to interfere in his administrative policies.

The reaction of the Hindus to such actions can be better understood if we examine their behaviour in connection with the second rebellion of Jujhar Singh Bundela, and the subsequent Imperial action at Orchha. Jujhar Singh was a rebel and no doubt he had to be punished and like Khan Jahan Lodi he got the punishment he deserved. But the Emperor's proceedings at Orchha—to which Prince Aurangzeb stood as a witness—could not but have left some lasting impressions on his mind. The Orchha incident was important, on the one hand it exposed the religious fanaticism of Shahjahan and on the other cowardice and indifference for the Hindu chiefs towards the fate of their own kinsmen and religion for power and prestige. At Orchha "the Islam cherishing Emperor demolished the grand temple built by Bir Singh near his palace and errected a mosque at it site."[7] "To this Devi Singh, the newly appointed Raja, made no objection. The temples of his gods might be defiled, his brave and proud clansmen might be butchered, the princesses of his house might be dragged into a shame worst than death–but he could

---

7. *ibid.*, I, ii, pp. 121-122. Orchha was occupied in October 1635 and Devi Singh was installed as the Raja of Orchha, while Jujhar Singh with his son Vikramajit and his family had escaped to Dhamuni. The Imperial forces continued their chase after the rebel chief and his followers. The Bundela chief escaped into the Gond country of Deogarh and Chanda were Jujhar Singh and Vikramajit were murdered by the Gonds and their

(*Contd. on page* 205)

now sit on the throne of Orchha and call himself a Raja and the head of the Bundela clan and therefore he rejoiced."[8] Among the Hindu Rajputs who were loyal to the Mughal Emperor and assisted or witnessed these pious acts of the Emperor were Raja Jai Singh Kachhwaha, Raja Jagat Singh Sisodia, Vithaldas Gaur, Kishan Singh Bhaduriya, Narhardas Jhala and may others.[9] Remarking on the attitude of these Rajput chiefs Dr. Saksena says, "The Hindu officers in his employ, though some of them were not lacking in courage, were smaller in number, lower in ranks, and hopelessly degenerate in character ... They held power and position dearer than the honour and sacredness of their religion."[10]

To young Aurangzeb the proceedings at Orchha left an everlasting impression. He must have wondered the indifference of the Rajputs at the insults showered on their religion, and must have made his assessment that the Rajputs were no hinderence to the state in following an orthodox religious policy, so long as their personal rank and position remained unaffected. He must have also realised that among the Rajput

---

severed heads were sent to the Emperor who had by then reached Saihur where these heads were exposed at the gate of the camp. In the process of pursuit a number of children and women had fallen into the hands of the Imperial forces. These woman were sent as slaves into the Imperial harem where they spent the rest of their life in ignomini. Three male captives of tender age—two sons and one grandson of Jujhar Singh...were converted to Islam. Prince Aurangzeb who was then working as the Imperial representative with a nominal supreme command had requested the Emperor to visit the area. The Emperor reached Orchha towards the end of November, 1635.

8. Sarkar, *History of Aurangzeb* Vol. I (1912), p. 29.
9. *Badshah Nama*, I, ii, pp. 96-7, 99-100, Lahori has given the names of these chiefs.
10. B. P. Saksena, *History of Shahjahan of Dihli*, p. 90.

chiefs there was no dirth of claiments who would assist in any fanatical action of the state only if he was assured of an improvement in his personal position. With these lessons Aurangzeb moved southwards with the Emperor and after the submission of the rulers of Bijapur and Golkunda while the Emperor returned to the north, Aurangzeb was appointed as the Viceroy of the Deccan in July 1636 at the age of eighteen and remained in that capacity till 1644.

While Aurangzeb remained in the Deccan, Dara Shukoh at Agra gradually began to gain prestige and position. His proximity to the Emperor made him powerful and gradually he began to control the administration. His ascendency was secretly resented by Aurangzeb, who began to feel that he was not only being neglected but because of Dara's influence his requests were either rejected or not properly attended It is said that he got so much disgusted with his position that he finally resigned from his post as a protest against Dara's persistent hostility and Shahjahan's partiality to Dara depriving him of the Emperor's confidence and support. Abdul Hamid Lahori says that he wanted to take to the retired life of an ascentic and had also done some acts which the Emperor disapproved of and therefore he was removed from service as a punishment. Khafi Khan says "to anticipate his father's punishment of the bad deeds he himself resigned and lived for some days as a harmit."[11] Bernier also speaks of the inci-

11. Sarkar, *Loc. cit.*, i, p. 76.
On page 78 Sarkar has pointed out that, "Turning recluse" (*manzavi ikhtiar kardan*) is a phrase commonly used in the Persian histories of India to mean the laying down of (Military) rank, office, and uniform in such a manner as not to imply a defiance of the Emperor's wishes. We often read how an officer under Imperial displeasure who had "turned hermit" in this sense, was afterwards reinstated in the rank and office on recovering his master's grace.

dent though in a restrospective judgement he assessed this ascetic strain in the character of Aurangzeb as hypocritical.[12] In reality the ambition to ascend the throne and jealousy for Dara was burning in his heart from the very begining and he was worried about the ascendency and proximity of Dara and may be, he wanted some time to contemplate on the future course of action.

Shahjahan no doubt tried to assert the Islamic character of the state, but in actual practice he made a compromise between Muslim orthodoxy and Akbar's liberalism. May be, it was an outcome of Dara's increasing influence over the Emperor and the administration; or may be, it was Emperor's own realisation that compromise between the extremes was demanded by the expediency of the time. However, the compromise set in motion two tendencies, one liberal and the other orthodox, and became manifest in the respective personalities of Dara and Aurangzeb.

Dara Shukoh possessed the intellectual strain of Akbar. "In his thirst for pantheistic philosophy he has studied the Talmud and the New Testament, the writings of Muslim sufis and the Hindu Vedanta. With the help *pandits* he had made a Persian version of the Upanishads. The title of *Majuma-ul-Baharain* (*the Mingling of two Oceans*) which he gave to another of his works, as well as his perfatory remarks prove that his aim was to find a meeting-point between Hinduism and Islam in those universal truths which form the common basis of all true religions and which fanatics are too apt to ignore in their zeal for mere externals of faith. But he was no apostate from Islam."[13] "The correct assessment of his spirituality," writes Aziz Ahmad, "seems to be that though his mind was imprgnated by Hinduism, he remained a convinced Muslim."[14] As a result of Dara's personal views the

12. Bernier, *Travels etc.*, p. 13.
13. Sarkar, *Loc. cit.* i, pp. 996-7.
14. Aziz Ahmad, *Islamic Culture in the Indian Environment*, p. 195.

orthodox section was apprehensive that his succession to the throne would result in the reversion to Akbar's concept of state in which they had experienced that they could hardly get any undue favours.

Aurangzeb as Viceroy of the Deccan realised that his future success against Dara depended much upon the opinion that he could muster in his favour. The non-orthodox section was already attached to Dara but the orthodox elements found no encouragement from him. Aurangzeb could visualise that his own leanings towards orthodoxy if ventilated through his action would atonse divert the attention of the orthodox section towards him. He could understand that Muslim consensus at that stage was divided, and a section was keen to preserve Islamic identity through a re-orientation towards orthodox formalism and religio-political particularism which stood quite opposed to Dara's religious syncretism. Of course, Aurangzeb was fully conscious that the ultimate decision rested in the final test of strength and was aware of the importance of support at the Imperial court. As a youth he had witnessed the way in which his father's accession was brought about. Once convinced Aurangzeb steadily went on taking steps to highlight his stand and even to display his personal orthodoxy that stood in marked contrast with Dara. It is in this context that we should view his destruction of the temple of Khande Rai at Satara and the temple of Chintaman close to Sarashpur ; observation of orthodox practices such as discarding cushions, use of silver and gold vessels and abandoning of the use of silk in his private life. His letter to Sa'adulla Khan asking him to prevent the appeal of the brothers of Chhabila Ram for the wrongful execution of their brother by the orders of Qazi Muhammad Maula and Shaikh Abul Mani the provincial sadr of Bihar, from reaching the Emperor.[15] This

15. Sarkar, Loe. cit., i, pp.173-4.

The letter reads "...I therefore remind you of this affair, as it is proper for all Muslim to do their utmost

(*Contd. on page* 209)

letter indicates that Aurangzeb had established his reputation as a protector of orthodoxy and had his admirers in different parts of the Empire, sot hat Mulla Muhan from Bihar appraised him of a situation which was well outside his administrative jurisdiction. It also gives an idea of the type of justice that the Hindus could except from him.

Aurangzeb was well aware of the character of the nobility both Muslim and Rajput. So far as the Rajputs were concerned he had not forgotten what he had seen earlier at Orchha and knew that allurement of promotion or providing an opportunity to avenge some wrong in the past was enough to gain their support. The Muslim nobility was equally undependable and would not hesitate to change sides at the slightest turn of fortune. All these made Aurangzeb cautious and led him keep his desire for throne a closely guarded secret. He always prepared to wait to strike at the opportune moment rather than to move in haste. When Shahjahan bestowed on Dara the title of *Shahi-i-buland iqbal* : increased his rank from 40 thousand *zat* to 60 thousand and raised him almost to royal position in rank and previledges, it became clear that he wished to leave the crown to Dara without bothering much for his other sons.[16] Shahjahan had obviously

to assert the rules of the Prophet's religion, and it is duty of the kings and nobles to protect the scholars of Islam in enforcing the injunctions of the Holy Law. You should exert yourself more than your peers to close the road of complaint of this wretched tribe to the Emperor's feet and take care of letters of guardians of the honour of the Faith.'—For the text of the letter, see *Adab-i-Alamgiri*, MS., Khuda Bakhash Library, Patna, fol. 101 a.

16. According to Muhammad Waris (*Badshahnama*) the title of *Shah-i-buland iqbal* was bestowed on Dara on 3rn Feb,, 1655 ; Muhammad Salih Kambu (*Amal-i-Salih*) mentions that within two years Dara was promoted first to 50,000 and finally to 60,000 *zat* rank.

forgotton the precedence he had set before his sons in getting the crown for himself. Thus the arrangement made by Shahjahan was unlikely to be accepted by his sons as the final settlement. However, as an astute politician, Aurangzeb had noticed that Shuja and Murad were as much jealous of Dara's position and power as he himself was. In this hatred towards their elder brother Aurangzeb discovered a common bond and decided to maintain cordial relations with Murad and Shuja for future struggle. To keep Shnja in good humour he did not hesitate to betroth his daughter to Prince Zainul Abidin, son of Shuja, and in exchange had his son Muhammad Sultan betrothed to the daughter of Shuja, knowing that Shuja and his son were Shia.

In fact the three brothers had come to a mutual understannding and formed a league against Dara long before the struggle for throne began. They were keeping regular contact with each other from their respective postings with a view to take joint action in case of emergency

When in September 1657 Shahjahan suddenly fell ill and his condition began to worsen, the omens of trouble could be discerned by the wise. The news of the Emperor's serious condition spread like wild fire and led to great consternation among the officers of the state as they could see the imminent trouble. The three brothers after a brisk correspondence between each other felt that the time for joint action had come. In the course of exchange of letters Aurangzab took all possible cautions and did not give the slighest indication of many of the things he was plannning, and hypocritically advised Murad to observe caution. In one of his letters to Murad he wrote, "I understand that the influence of the enemy in administration has attained undesirable proportions. He is now trying to collect treasure and army......We should be very cautious at this time and should not write anything undesirable in our letters."[17] Though Shahjahan recovered by the middle of November 1657, the rumour had done

17. Saksena, *Loc. cit.*, p. 325.

its mischief. The Princes could not be convinced of the rocovery of their father. All such news was considered as mechinations of Dara to gain time. In haste, Murad and Shuja declared independence and proclaimed themselves as king. But Aurangzeb remained quiet. As an astuate politician he could foresee that in future two kings were bound to clash and would seek his help which would only fecilitate his design. He was not sure of his success and was wise enough to hide his real aim. He knew that religious slogan wou'd antagonise the Shias and as well may estrange the feelings of Shuja. Following the strategy, he next entered into a bargain with Rana Raj Singh Sisodia of Mewar——that for his assistance he would restore the parganas of Mandalgarh and its four mahals which Shahjahan had detached from his territory and if he comes out successful then the pargana of Idar would also be granted to him.[18] Aurangzeb even tried to seduce Jaswant Singh before the battle of Dharmat (April 1658). The personal views of Aurangzeb *vis-a-vis* Dara were already well known to the Muslims of India.[19] The victory at Dharmat was a turning point in the War of Succession. On the one hand it brightened the future prospects of Aurangzeb and on the other it vindicated his reputation as a military commander. The waverers could now see the future victor and began to rally round his banner.

The victory at Dharmat was followed by the victory at Samugarh and paved the way for Aurangzeb to the throne, But he had still to deal with his brother Murad who was with him as his partner at Samugarh and Shuja who was still roam-

18. *Vir Vinod*, ii, p. 420
19. The view once expressed by Maulana Shibli that "Aurangzeb rallied the Muslims together and fought for the throne." has already been put to test and demolished by Athar Ali, and need not be unnecessarily dialated upon. The plain truth is that for Aurangzeb there was no need of it. See ;
Proceedings Indian History Congress, 1960,

ing in the east. Therefore, Aurangzeb had to be cautious. Fortunately for Aurangzeb, Murad had been wounded in the battle of Samugarh and was out of action for a few weeks. Yet to beguile his brother and his followers, he behaved like a loving elder brother.[20] The victorious army was welcomed at Agra from where Dara had already left for Delhi. At Agra Shahjahan's efforts to reconcile Aurangzeb failed because his partisans impressed upon htm that the Emperor's reconciliatory move was only a ruse to arrest him. Aurangzeb after occupying the city besiegd the fort, which soon had to surrender.

It was at this time that Jahanara visited Aurangzeb in her bid to reconcile her brother and also expressing the wish of the Emperor to partition the empire among the brothers, giving to Aurangzeb the core of the empire as his share. Aurangzeb knew that the odds were in his favour and yet he could not dare to refuse outright everything to his elder sister for whom he had respect and regard and before her personality he had always stood in awe. With Emperor a virtual captive, Dara at Delhi, Murad present in his camp, Shuja holding himself in the east and his elder sister pleading for peace with a proposal for partition of the empire Aurangzeb found himself in a most critical situation. He was not prepared for sharing the empire, but could not declare it openly. He aimed at getting rid of each sharer by turn. Dara was his first target, and his earlier plea that Dara did not permit him to perform his duties properly, and obstructed his way to pay a visit to his father for which he was marching northwards, now became untenable under the altered situa-

20. Aurangzeb consoled Murad by saying that the victory was entirely due to his valour, and also that Murad's reign would date from that day. Khafi Khan mentions, may be satirically, that while the doctors were examining the wounds, Aurangzeb laid the head of Murad on his own knees, wiped the blood with his own sleeves, and wept pathetically at the sight. Who could have then suspected what was actually in the mind of Aurangzeb ?

tion. His earlier stand that he only wanted a replacement in the council of Shahjahan had to be changed. So he took recourse to the religious plea, and told his sister that, "Dara is an infidel to Islam and a friend to the Hindus, he must be extirpated for the sake of True Faith and the peace of the realm. I cannot visit the Emperor before concluding the business.',[20a] Aurangzeb then discovered that his father, though a virtual prisoner, was secretly making efforts to restore Dara, he, therefore, placed Shahjahan under stricter captivity and all communications between him and outside world was stopped.

At Agra, Aurangzeb gave grand audience to the public and received homage from the high officers of the state. Ranks were distributed at his command and fresh appointments were made. Aurangzeb emperor in all but name. But what about Murad ? His consellors instigated him and aroused in him a jealousy. Was it to promote Aurangzeb to the throne that he had bled ? What guarantee was there that Aurangzeb would give him his share according to earlier agreement ? But Murad could not see that his brother was already master of the situation and wisdom demanded concilation and not defiance. He should have known that Aurangzeb was not to be cowed down by defiance. Murad not only stopped visiting the brother but also set up a parallel court and started distributing *mansab* and appointing officers. But Murad was no match for Aurangzeb, by these actions he only created greater confusion. While Aurangzeb had to start for Delhi, Murad followed in order to prevent his brother from occupying the capital and its treasury all by himself. To get rid of Murad, Aurangzeb readly formed a plan. On the way to Delhi, Murad was imprisoned by Aurangzeb "through excellent strategem" and sent to the prison of Salimgarh without his followers knowing anything about it. The entire establishment of Murad became Aurangzeb's property. Murad's son Izid Bakhsh was sent to share his father's captivity.

20a. Aqil Khan Razi, *Waqiat-i-Alamgiri*, pp. 59-61.

After getting rid of Murad, Aurangzeb resumed his march to Delhi and reached there in July. Dara had already left Delhi on receiving the information of his brother's march in that direction. Aurangzeb now decided not to delay any longer in openly declaring his position as emperor, and on 21st July, 1658 had himself coronated. While military operations against Dara, Sulaiman Shukoh and Shuja continued, Aurangzeb transferred Murad and his son to the state prison of Gwalior in January 1659. Between July 1658 and June 1659, Aurangzeb defeated Shuja at Khajwa and Dara at Deorai and had thus vindicated his position as supreme among his brothers. It was time for him now to get himself recognised as the Emperor *de facto* and *de jure*. Thus in June 1659 Aurangzeb directed the Chief Qazi of the Empire to recite the *khutba* in his name on the occasion of his second or The Grand Coronation (5th June 1659) at Delhi. But the Chief Qazi pointed out that it was "not allowed in the Holy Religion to recite the *khutba* in the name of the son during the lifetime of the father". His majesty under these circumstances got worried. Qazi Abdul Wahab Gujrati Pattani represented to His Majesty that if he is "beneficiently instructed, he will convince the Chief Qazi to recite the holy *khutba* in the name of His Majesty. He was ordered that it would be an occasion for payment of homage. The shaikh declared that Shahjahan has become very weak. He has lost his consciousness. He had lost control over administrative machinery of the Empire. Recitation of the *khutba* under these circumstances, in the name of the son who is worthy of the *sultanat* and the *khilafat* is permissible and allowable in the Holy Religion He recited many reliable traditions in this respect before the Chief Qazi, and other *ulma* and scholors".[21]

The situation through which Aurangzeb had to pass to get the *Khutba* recited in his name made it clear to him that he must have a group of *ulama* on his side to give the verdict in

21. *Mirat-i-Ahmadi,* Eng. tr., p. 220.

his favour whenever occasion so demanded. Qazi Abdul Wahab was promoted to the post of *Qazi-ul-Quzat* (Chief Qazi) of the empire, as a reward for his giving turns and twists to declare the reading of the *khutba* in the name of Aurangzeb as valid. This gave encouragement to the *ulama*, who could see that the new Emperor was particular to get his actions stamped by a religious verdict. The reason of this orthodoxy was perhaps due to the fact that Dara was still alive and Aurangzeb was out to pacify the orthodox section to gain their support. However, the religious plea once taken up had to be buttressed by positive measures to assure the orthodox element of the line of policy he was going to follow. It is in consonance with this aim that Aurangzeb issued a number of ordinnnces immediately after his coronation. These ordinances were : (1) Stamping of the *kalima* on the coins was forbidden lest the holy words be trampled under-foot or defiled by the unbeleivers ; (2) The Nauroz festival was to be discontinued and its court rejoicings were to be merged with the coronation festivity ; (3) A *Muhtasib* was appointed to regluate the lives of the people in strict accordance with the Holy Law. "The innovators, atheists, hyprocrites who had spread over India were chastised and forced to give up their wicked courses and were forced to obey the theologians and observe the fasts and prayers regularly."[22] (4) Cultivation of *bhang* was prohibited throughout the empire ; (5) All old mosque and monastries, in and around Delhi were repaired and made as new ; (6) *Imams, muazzins, Khatibs* and *khadims* were appointed with regular salaries; and students were granted daily allowances so that they could engage in the study of theology with composure of mind.[23] To the orthodox sections these measures

22. Aqil Khan, quoled Sarkar, *Aurangzeb*, iii, p. 93.

23. *ibid* , p. 95. The amount spent on this item alone can be judged from a reference tn the ninth year of Aurangzeb's reign when we are told that it cost the state one lakh rupees every year to maintain the 600 mosques at Delhi.

were of great importance. In these, they discovered the future possibilities of their position in the affairs of state.

By 15th of July Aurangzeb was relieved of the first anxiety when he received the news of Dara's captivity from his officer Bahadur Khan. He immediately ordered that Dara and his son should be paraded through the bazars of Delhi before they were confined to the prison. His aim was that people should see "with their own eyes that it was Dara and none else so that in future no counterfeit Dara might raise his head in the provinces and by winning support of the credulous create disturbances." On the 29th August Dara was paraded through the bazars of Delhi and then lodged in Khwaspur mansion outside Shahjahanabad.

"The same evening the fate of Dara was debated in the Hall of Private Audience. A small section of the nobles pleaded for his life, but the majority of them demanded his death. The malignant influence of his younger sister Roshanara was thrown in the scale against Dara, and her clamours silenced the feeble voice of mercy in a Court where most ministsrs shaped their opinions after their master's inclinations. The pliant theologians in the Emperor's pay signed a decree that Dara deserved death on the ground of infidelity and deviation from Islamic orthodoxy,"[24] The execution of Dara was an outcome of political ambition of Aurangzeb, who could never feel himself safe so long Dara lived but the official charge sheet framed against Dara was based on the religious plea.[25] Once such a plea was taken

---

24. Sarkar, *Aurangzeb*, ii, pp. 213-14
25. *Alamgir Nama*, pp. 34-35, Muhammad Kazim gives the official charge sheet : "Dara Shukoh in has later days on account of his misfortune and inauspiciousness did not confine himself to infldelity and heresy alone, which were inherent in his nature and which he had named *Tasawwuf*, but also showed an inclination towards the religion of the Hindus and institution of accursed ones. He was constantly in the society of the *Brahmins*, *Jogis*

and the order of execution carried out, the damage to the state policy had been done beyond reparation. Henceforth Aurangzeb could not give up this line, because a little deviation would expose him to the same charges which had been levelled against his political rival and elder brother.

Aurangzeb got rid of Dara but yet he was not free from the danger. Shuja was still alive and lurking for a suitable opportunity to strike; Sulaiman Shukoh was yet to be captured and above all to his surprise he discovered that his own son Muhammad Sultan was fraternising with his uncle Shuja. Thus the enemies that he was called upon to face were all his relations and belonged to the same faith. He had to be very

---

and *Sanayasis* and used to regard this crowd of prevaricators, misguided ones and the worthless fellows as perfect guides and *Arif* who had reached God. He considers their books which they call Veda as being divine, and the word of God, revealed from heaven and the most ancient and venerable of books. Under such misbelief and delusion abont the worthless *Veda*, he collected *Brahmins* and *Sanyasis* from all parts of the country with great efforts, and paying them great attention and care, he employed them in translating the *Veda*. He spent all his time in this unholy work, and devoted all his attention to the contents of these wretched books. Instead of the sacred name of God he adopted the Hindawi name *Prabhu* and had this name eneraved in his seal ring. It became manifest that if he obtained the throne and estabiished supreme power and authority, the pillars of *Shariat* would be in danger and the precepts of Islam would be changed for infidelity." "The pillars of the Canonical Law and Faith apprehended many kinds of disturbance from his life. So the Emperor, both out of necessity to protect the Faith and Holy Law, and also for reasons of state, considered it unlawful to allow Dara to remain alive any longer as a destroyer of the public peace."

careful in taking measures against them because a little mistake or oversight could prove disasterous for him. Shuja was finally defeated and pushed into Bengal hotly pursued by Mir Jumla, who ultimately drove him out of Bengal into the hostile regions inhabited by the Maghs. Muhammad Sultan in the meantime had been imprisoned as a punishment for his crime. Early in January 1661 Sulaiman Shukoh was also brought as a prisoner to Delhi, and was finally sent as a prisoner to the state prison of Gwalior on the pious oath of the God-fearing Emperor that slow poison would not be administered to him, and, yet such was the secret instruction of the Emperor to the gaoler that *pousta* drink should be regularly administered to him.[26]

Aurangzeb should have been mentally free after this, but a smooth sailing as Emperor was not destined to him. In the fourth year of his reign a plot to rescue Murad Bakhsha from

26. Bernier who was an eye witness has given a vivid account of proceedings : "Many of the courtiers shed tears at the sight of this interesting young man........... The principal ladies of the court, concealed behind a lattice work were greatly moved. Aurangzeb spoke with kindness, 'Be conforted ; no harm shall befall you. You shall be treated with tenderness. God is great, and you should put your trust in Him. Your father was not permitted to live only beeause he had become a *kafir*.' The Prince made the *salam*..... and told the Emperor that if it were intended to give him *pousta* to drink, he begged that he might immediately be put to death Aurangzeb promised in a solemn manner, and in loud voice, that this drink should most certainly not be administered, and that his mind might be perfectly easy." But Aurangzeb in violation of his solemn promise ordered the captive to be plied with the drink of opium-seed In this condition Sulaiman Shukoh dragged his life moving slowly towards death under the influence of the drink till in May 1662 he died.

the prison of Gwalior was discovered. Though the plot failed but Aurangzeb realised the danger and decided to get rid of him. But for such an action a pretext had to be found out, and for Aurangzeb it was not a difficult task. Murad was executed on the charge of the murder of Ali Naqi, the provincial diwan of Gujarat[27], on 4th December, 1661.

The execution of Murad was an outcome of political necessity, but to maintain a show of justice, recourse to religious law had been taken. As a further proof of glorifying Islam during this period, Daud Khan destroyed many temples in Palamau and similarly Mir Jumla destroyed a number of temples in Kuch Bihar and after destroying the idols converted them into mosques.[28] The process of distruction of temples had started in the reign of Shahjahan and there was nothing new in such measures but now it was taken as pious acts of Aurangezeb which during the ascendency of Dara had been discontinued. So far the Hindus were concerned such acts had ceased to hurt their sentiments. They had by then accepted such activities as an inseperable part of the Muslim rule, and believed that it was a part of their destiny and the sufferings were due to their mis-deeds in their past life.

The manner in which Aurangzeb brought about his usurpation of the throne and the treatment he meted out to his

27. At the instigation of Aurangzeb, the second son of Ali Naqi lodged a complaint in the law court seeking justice against the murder of his father. Aurangzeb directed the Qazi of Gwalior to decide the case according to the evidence and the Quranic Law. The plaintiff arrived at court and opened his case before the Qazi. Murad could see through the game and refused to defend himself. Qazi convicted Murad and as the avenger refused to accept blood-money, death sentenee was pronounced according to Islamic Law. On 4th December, 1661 Murad was executed.
28. Sri Ram Sharma, *The Religious Policy* etc. (1940) p 137.

brothers and particularly to his father started affecting his reputation both within the country and outside. His first step to counter act such reactions was to cover every thing in a shower of gold. Immediately after his Grand Coronation he had sent Mir Ibrahim with six lakhs and sixty thousand rupees for distribution among pious person at Macca and Medina. According to Manucci, holy men of Macca declined to accept the gifts sent by Aurangzeb because his father was still alive, but subsequently the Grand Sharif of Macca decided to accept it.[29] He found in this pious act of the Emperor a regular source of income, which even Aurangzeb later in his reign started resenting. The correspondence with Shah Abbas II of Persia in which Aurangzeb dilates the narrative of his triumphs over his brothers, and includes self-righteous declaration that he was devoting every hour of his life to doing good to his subjects, promoting peace and prosperity in the land and advancing the cause of Islam, clearly indicate that he was only advancing an explanation for his occupying the throne.

Aurangzeb, no doubt had an orthodox bent of mind, but when he found himself put in a situation where justification of his action was necessary to recover public respect. which had suffered due to his action against his father, "he posed as the champion of Islamic orthodoxy, as the reluctant and compelled instrument of the divine will in a mission of much needed religious reform. Hence he displayed extreme zeal in restoing the ordinances of pure Islam and removing heretical innovations, so that people might forget his past conduct as a son and as a brother, till at last his court historian could write of him : "*Hisi mperial robe of state thinly veiled the darvish's frock that he wore beneath it.*"[30]

Once Aurangzeb started posing as the champion of Islamic orthodoxy, it was not possible for him to retrace his

29. Sarkar, *Auraugzeb*, iii, 117.
30. *ibid.*, p. 165.

steps, one action of orthodoxy had to be followed by another before the lustre of the first got dull under the stress of time. He inaugurated the Eighth year of his reign by showing special favour to the Muslims. By a Royal Order issued on 10th April 1665 the custom duty on all commodities brought for sale was fixed at $2\frac{1}{2}\%$ of the value in case of the Muslims and 5% in that of the Hindu vendors. In the Nineth year Aurangzeb ordered for the removal of the stone railing in the temple of Keshava Rai at Mathura which had been presented by Dara, on the plea that in "the Muslim faith it is a sin even to look at a temple, and this Dara had restored a railing in a temple. This fact is not creditable to the Muslims".[31] The removal of the railing served double purpose ; while it assumed the shape of an act of piety of the Emperor, it also removed a relic which was associated with the name of Dara and was keeping his memory fresh.

Shivaji had escaped from Agra on 13th August 1666, but it would be wrong to associate such measures as retalitory steps against the Hindus. The other direction which we generally overlook was the threat of Persian invasion on the Punjab and for meeting which an army was sent on 25th August 1666. It was a critical situation and Aurangzeb needed greater support for meeting an enemy who was also a Muslim. Thus something had to be done to stress the Islamic character of his state so as to rally the orthodox sentiments on his side as against Shicite Persians. Though the Persian invasion did not take place, but in March 1667 the Yusufzai uprising in Peshawar created a new situation and the Emperor had to send reinforcement to suppress the uprising. To gain greater support of the Muslims and to appeal to their sentiments the Emperor took a new step. On 9th May 1667 he abolished the custom duty altogether in case of the Muslims though on the Hindus it was retained at the same level of 5%. This was a greater discriminatory measure against the Hindus

31. *Akhbarat,* 9th Year sheet (14th October, 1666) *vide,* Sarkar, *Aurangzeb*, iii, p. 320.

but none raised a voice of protest. Mirza Raja Jai Singh Kachwaha, Raja Jaswant Singh Rathore and the whole host of Hindu and Rajput chiefs in the employ of the state did not dare to raise their finger to point out to the Emperor that such a measure was not fair to the Hindus. *Probably they too felt that it was the minority who should enjoy the fruits of the labour of the majority under a good government of a minority.* This measure of Aurangzeb positively indicates his efforts to stress the Islamic character of the state in which only the Believers were entitled to enjoy the benefits from the state. But in its practical application the state was deprived of the revenue it derived from the Muslims ; and it led the Hindu traders to get their goods passed as the property of the Muslims who did not hesitate to co-operate with the Hindus on this matter. That Aurangzeb was not aware of such a possibility cannot be sustained because the order itself incorporates a warning to the officers against such a fraud.[32] In the eleventh year of his reign Aurangzeb forbade the musicians from playing music in the court. *No wonder the Darvesh's frock began to peep from below the Imperial robe.* But by this measure Aurangzeb must have saved some amount in the court expenditure.

In the 12th year of his reign, Aurangzeb issued orders (April, 9, 1669) to "the governors of all the provinces to demolish the schools and temples of the infidels and strongly put down their teaching and religious practices."[33] It becomes difficult to find out exactly the motive of Aurangezeb in issuing a general order effecting the entire length and the breadth of his empire. No doubt, he had issued orders earlier prohibiting construction of new temples and repair of the old ones. By prohibiting repair he had expected that the old ones would crumble down in course of time, but most probably his orders were not strictly observed and this irritated the Emperor and convinced him of the laxiety and easy-

32. *Mirat-i-Ahmadi*, Eng. tr., p. 237.
33. *Ma'asir-i-Alamgiri*, p. 81, quoted Sarkar, iii-321.

going habit of his officers. The allegation that the temples were used as schools which attracted students, both Hindus and Muslims seems to be doubtful. Should we believe that the Hindus had shaken off their orthodoxy so as to allow the Muslims to enter the prscinets of their timples and teach them their sacred books. If such was the real picture, it meant that the two communities had come very close to each other, which scared the Emperor that unless the process was put to a stop the Muslims would soon loose their identity. We may take note that the Muslims used the mosque as a place where their children received education, and, similarly the Hindus used the temple premises as school for their children. This was an old custom which had continued down through the ages. Should we then presume that by this order Aurangzeb wanted the Hindus to remain uneducated, or that he wanted the Hindu system of education to be entirely given up in his empire, or that he believed, that, if the Hindus remain ignorant of their own religion they would easily embrace Islam. But none of these explanations satisfy the situation, and it has to wait for an intellectual speculation of a modern genius to probe into the mind of Aurangzeb for a satisfactory answer. Whatever the motives of Aurangzeb might have been but his order that "report of the destruction of temples should be sent to the court under the seal of the *qazis* and attested by pious shaikhs"[34] must have been very irritating to the officers because such an order subordinated them to the *qazi* and the theologians.

As a result of this order, the Vishwanath temple of Varanasi was demolished sometimes in August, 1669[35] and in its place a mosque was built. The temple of Gopi Nath at Varanasi was also demolished about the same time.[36]

In the 13th year of Aurangzeb's reign, Keshava Rai temple at Mathra built by Bir Singh Bundela at a cost of

34. Sharma, *Religious Policy of the Mughals*, p. 138.
35. *Ma'asir-i-Alamgiri*, p. 88.

Rs. 33,00,000 was raised to the ground. The idols studded with precious stones and adorned with gold works, were taken to Agra and there burried under the steps of Jahanara's mosque. Though the official historian is silent but we can safely presume that the idols must have been first stripped off all its valuables like precious stones and gold works which must have supplied some return to the state. On the site of Keshava Rai temple it was ordered that a mosque should be built to mark the acquisition of religious merit by the emperor.[37] The proceedings at Mathura scared the priests at Vrindavana who evacuated the place and carried with them the idols and moving from place to place ultimately succeeded in getting an assylum in a neglected corner of Rana Raj Singh's territory at Sihar which subsequently became famous as Nathdwara and Udaipur became a centre of northern Vaishnavism.[38]

The general order of Aurangzeb for the distruction of temples and closing of schools stood in sharp contrast with

36. It May be noted that in 1669 Aurangzeb had issued a *farman* to Abul Hasan, in which he had stated : "It has been decided according to our Cannon Law (*Shariat*) that long standing temples should not be demolished but no new temples be allowed to be built. The Royal Court has received information that some persons are troubling the Hindus and some Brahmins in and about Banaras, who had been granted the right of worship in the old temples. They are trying that these Brahmins should be deprived of their hereditary right of worship. Our Royal command is that you should direct that in future no person shall, in unlawful ways, interfere with or disurtb the Brahmins and other Hindu residents in those places." *vide Farman* of Aurangzeb dated 28-2-1659, Bharat Kala Bhawan, Varanasi.

37. *Ma'asir-i-Alamgiri*, pp. 95-6 ; Manucci, ii, p. 116.

38. Sharma,, *Religious policy* etc. p. 142.

the religious policy of Akbar. This order made the Mughal statè a sectarian state, the benefits of which were to go to the Muslims alone ; the majority of tax-payers i.e. the Hindus were reduced to the position of mere instruments for providing means of enjoyment to the minority.

The general order for destruction of temples was followed by another order for putting the Hindus at a disadvantageous position. In 1671 the Emperor issued orders that Hindus were not to be employed in the revenue department as assistants to various heads.[39] This orders though sought to provide employment at lower levels to the Muslims it failed to achieve its object because the Muslims were more interested in military career, where promotion to higher positions was easier. Of course as a result of this order many Hindus in the revenue department changed their faith to Islam.[40] If the addition to the Muslim population could afford some satisfaction to the Emperor he should have felt happy for taking such a wise step. In the rank of mansabdars above 1000 a decline in the number of Hindu encumbents is perceptible. Though there is a marked incr:ase in the totnl number of mansabdars we do not find a proportionate increase in number of the Hindu mansabdars.[41]

By degrees Aurangzeb did succeed in giving a pronounced Islamic appearance to the Mughal state. Between 1659 and 1670 he discontinued the institutions of *Jharokha-i-Darshan* and birthday - weighing in gold. But strangely enough, the Islamic character that he was endevouring to give to the Moghul state in India did not solve his problems. The

---

39. *Ma'asir-i-Alamgiri,* p. 528 ; Khafi Khan, ii, p. 249 ; *Kalimat-i-Tayyibat.*
40. Khafi Khan, ii. p. 252.
41. In recent times attempts are being made to show that there was increase in the Hindu mansabdars. But if we examine the tables and calculate the dead ones we will find that such was not the case.

problems came not from the Hindus but from the Muslims. Between 1672 and 1675 he was called upon to tackle the Afridi uprising which seriously exposed the Mughal might. In the frontier operations Muhammad Amin Khan was defeated and disgraced (April, 1672), Shujait Khan was slain in the Karapa pass (Feb. 21, 1674), Mukarram Khan met disaster in the Bajaur country (June 1675). The uprising of the Afghan tribesmen was subdued but at a high price both in men and money. The frontier problems was not solved by finding a permanent solution but by following "the policy of paying subsidies and setting clan, against clan or by breaking two bones by knocking them together. The Khybar route was kept open by paying regular pension to the hillmen."[42] This Afghan war heavily drained the Imperial finances. Its political effect was even more ruinous. The operations in frontier "relieved the pressure on Shivaji by draining the Deccan of its best Mughal troops for putting them on the frontier. The Maratha chief took advantage of this diversion to sweep in a dazzling succession of triumphs through Golkunda to the Karnatik and back again through Bijapur territory to Raigharh, during the eighteen months following December 1676. It was the climax of his career ; but the Afridis and Khataks made its unbroken success possible."[43]

To meet the heavy expenditure the Emperor again took shelter in the Drvesh's frock. In Novemer 1677 i.e. beginning of the 21st year of his reign the Emperor introduced puritanical simplicity into his court. The customary rejoicings at the anniversary of his coronation were abolished. Betel leaves and scents were distributed among those present at Court, but the throne-room was henceforth furnished and upholstered in a cheap and simple style ; the clerks were to use porcelain inkpots instead of silver ones ; the money for the largesses was to be brought in on shields instead of silver

---

42. Sarkar, *Aurangzeb*, iii, p. 279
43. *ibid.*, iii, p. 282.

trays. In the department of robe of honour (khilat) cloth of gold embroidery was ordered to be used in the place of *butadar* ornamented with silver filigree. The railing of gold and silver in the Hall of Public Audience were pronounced uncanonical and replaced by railings of lapis lazuli set on gold.[44] These measures must have brought about a considerable economy for the treasury on account of Imperial establishment. Every step at economising the state expenditure was bound to effect the officers and therefore a religious colouring or the garb of puritanical simplicity had to be adopted. Every time the Emperor consulted the ulama their importance in the state was enhanced. Thus by the year 1678 Aurangzeb had practically taken all the possible steps to give the state Islamic character, the only step that remained to be taken was the imposition of *jaziya* to complete the picture.

The imposition of *jaziya* by Aurangzeb on 2nd April 1679 has already been a topic of controversy and scholars have tried to link it up with the death of Maharaja Jaswant Singh of Jodhpur.[45] The incidents that apparently link the two are as follows: Maharaja Jaswant Singh died at Jamrud on 10th December, 1678. He was then posted at the Thanadar of Jamrud and was in command of the Mughal forces posted in the Khybar pass and the district of Peshawar. The news reached the Emperor at Delhi in the fourth week of the month. At the time of his death Jaswant Singh was heavily in debt to the Imperial Treasury.

44. *ibid.*, iii, p. 99 ; See *Ma'asir-i-Alamgiri*, p. 98, 162.
45. Such a view was given currency first of all by Manucci and others have simply copied him. "The death of Jaswant Singh," writes Manucci, "was used by still Aurangzeb as an opening to oppress the Hindus more, since they had no longer any valiant or powerful rajah who could defend them. He imposed on the Hindus a poll-tax, which every one was forbed to pay." *vide*, Manucci, ii, 233-34.

The Emperor was informed that Jaswant Singh and his ancestors had hoarded treasure in the fort of Siwana. A search for the treasure was ordered but it yielded nothing. An ordered was issued in February 1679 that the entire property belonging to Jaswant Singh was to be escheated. In the mean time the Emperor himself had moved to Ajmer (started on 9th January, 1679) and had summoned Asad Khan, Shaista Khan and Prince Akbar from their provinces to reinforce the Imperial forces at Ajmer. The Emperor ordered that the entire state of Jodhpur except two parganas, was to be coverted into *khalisa* (Feb. 1679) and appointed Imperial *faujdar, qiladar, kotwal,* and *amin* for the annexed Jodhpur state. In the quest for hidden treasure Aurangzeb even appointed an officer to dig under the fort walls, new mansion and courtyards. While at Ajmer Aurangzeb received the news of the birth of two posthumous sons of Jaswant Singh. In March Aurangzeb seems to have been satisfied with arrangements made for the state of late Jaswant Singh and started for Delhi reaching there on 2nd April 1679 and on the same day *Jaziya* was imposed on the Hindus which had been kept in abeyance for a century. This was followed by accepting Indra Singh as the Raja of Jodhpur (May 26, 1679). This was followed by the confinement and subsequent escape of new born son and his mother through the efforts of Durgadas which ultimately resulted in the war with the Rothors.

The imposition of *Jaziya* and the Rothor rebellions are only coincidence and not causally connected with each other. If we see the details we will find that the opposition to the imposition of *jaziya* came from the Muslim nobles of Aurangzeb's court and also from Jahanara[46] but not from his Hindu nobles. The Rajputs were too much centred round in their personal interests to think anything about it. The view that so long Mirza Raja Jai Sing and Maharaja Jaswant lived Aurangzeb postponed the imposition of jaziya because he was afraid of Rajput resistance under the guidance of two

46. Manucci iii, pp. 274-275.

great chiefs is not tenable. As pointed out earlier even during the lifetime of these two chiefs, Aurangzeb was taking measure after measure to discrimate against the Hindus but neither Jai Singh nor Jaswant Singh ever raised any objection against such steps. In fact both these Rajput chiefs had become servile vassals of the Mughal Emperor. The destruction and descration of the religious places of the Hindus had taken place during their life-time and yet we do not find a single Rajput chief protesting against such acts. They continued to serve loyally and continued to enjoy the security of service. If we give any credence to the records contained in *Waqai Ajmer*, we find startling revealations about the attitude of the Rajputs. At one place it records that when Rani Hadi the chief queen of Jaswant Singh heard about the *Tika* was being proposed to be offered to Indra Singh, she declared if Jodhpur was conferred on the son of the late Raja, the Rajputs undertook to demolish all temples in the state of Marwar. At another place it records that Ram Bhati and Sonkar Rathor went to Kazi Hamid of Jodhpur and represented that if the *watan* and the *zamindari* was conferred on the son of the deceased Raja, the Rajputs undertook to demolish all temples of Jodhpur and construct mosques instead. The Rajputs were also prepared to promulgate the law of the *Shariat* and to caray out the orders of the Emperor to whataver effect. Yet at another place it records that Tahir Khan also reported in the same month to the Emperor that the Rajputs were prepared to demolish all temples within the Jodpur State, to promulgate Islam and to ofler a bigger *Peshkash* than that offered by Indra Singh, if the appointment of Indra Singh as Raja of Jodhpur was cancelled. On the face of it these records appear incredible, but if we recall the demolition of the temple at Orchha during the reign of Shahjahan and that too in the presence of so many Rajput chiefs belonging almost to all the important houses and the way Debi Singh assisted in these acts of sacrilege against his gods and the humiliation to the Bundela family merely for the sake of the *gaddi* of Orchha, one gets convinced that for the Rajputs what mattered was their *gaddi* and personal gain. Their religion failed to infuse in them that spirit which Islam infused among its believers. Sir Jadunath has very aptly compared the respective attitudes of the two communities towards their religion. "To contrast the Hindu spirit with the Muhammadan", writes Sir Jadunath, "let us consider an imaginary parallel. Suppose that when Clive after winning Plassey marched to Murshidabad and placed Mir Jafar on the throne, he had ordered the chief mosque of the town to be converted into a Christian Church, where pigs would be sacrificed every year on Atonement Day, would Mir Jafar have consented to take the crown on such a condition, would the Muslim troops in the East India Company's service have submitted to this insult to their religion ?"[47]

Thus we find that Aurangzeb was absolutely certain that whatever steps he might take to make the state based entirely on the lines of the *Shariat,* there would be no opposition from the Hindus who by then had become supine and completelty resigned to their lot of suffering and degradation. For Aurangzeb's extreme orthodox policy the Hindus were more responsible than the Emperor himself. If Aurangzeb had received opposition just when he launched his policy of discrimination against the Hindus, he might have reconsidered his measure and would have stopped at a certain point.

The motive of Aurangzeb in reimposing *jaziya* has been variously given by contemporary and near contemporary observers, but all of them in one from or other follow the line given by the official historian Saqi Mustaid Khan. The official history records : "As all the aims of the religious Emperor were directed to the spreading of the law of Islam and the overthrow of the practices of the infidels, he issued orders to the high diwani officers that from Wednesday, the 2nd April, 1679/1st Rabi I, in obedience to the Quranic injunction 'till they pay commutation money (*jaziya*) with

47. Sarkar, *Aurangzeb* p. 30, notes.

the hand in humility' and in agreement with the canonical traditions, *jaziya* should be collected from the infidels (*zimmis*) of the capital and the provinces. Many of the honest scholars of the time were appointed to discharge the work (of collecting *jaziya*).[48]

According to Ishwar Das, the theologians, the learned men and the traditionists in view of the regard of the Emperor for the True Faith, represented to him that levying of *jaziya* was necessary and compulsory according to *Shariat*[49]. Ali Muhammad Khan says, "As all the energy of His Majesty was direeted to strengthening the clear religion and giving currency to the usages of the strong Path, he moulded all state affairs and financial and revenue matters in the religious cast. Learned men, scholars and theologians saw that His Majesty encouraged religion during his auspicious regime, they represented to him the *levy* of *Jizya* on zimmis of the Empire necessary and incumbent in accordance with the path of bright religion and way of shining creed."[50]

While these writers have ascribed pure religious motives on the part of the Emperor, the Europeans in India have added something more. Thus according to Thomas Roll, President of Surat English Factory, *jaziya* was being collected with object of replinishing the Emperor's exhausted treasury and also of forcing the poorer sections of the population to become Muslims.[51] Writing on *jaziya* Manucci comments that Aurangzeb imposed it for two reasons; first because by this time (1679) his treasuries had begun to shrink owing to expenditure of his campaigns ; secondly to force Hindus to becomc Mohmmedans."[52]

---

48. *Ma'asir-i-Alamgiri* (Tr.) p. 108.
49. B. M. Ms. Add. 23814, fol. 74a.
50. *Mirat-i-Ahmadi*, (Tr.) p. 264.
51. *The English Factories in India*, ed. FaWcett, new Series, iii, p. 241.
52. Manucci, ii, p. 233-4 ; iii, p. 288.

There is much truth in whatever has been written by these observers. It was a number of factors that led Aurangzeb to re-impose *jaziya* and naturally observer may stress only that factor which to him seemed to be the factor. Similarly in the case of interpretation by modern writers different interpretations have been forwarded by them and according to their own understanding they have laid stress on one or the otheraspect. However one thing is definite that the imposition of *jaziya* completed the orthodox Islamic character of the state which was started by Aurangzeb with his accession to the throne.

The proceeds collected under the head of *jaziya* were deposited in a separate treasury known as *Khazanah-i-jaziyah* and was meant exclusively for distribution of charity and the beneficiaries were the *Ulama* and other muslim stipend holders. Thus the imposition of *jaziya* directly improved the condition of the clerical section in an uncertain economy of the empire, and by and large they became the supporters of the Emperor.

Thus Aurangzeb having started his reign with the plea of Islamic orthodoxy had to move on the same line taking one step after another and had to depend on the support of the orthodox section and the self seeking-ulama. The orthodox trend could call to its assistance the powerful forces of dogmatism which took little account of the situation prevailing at the time. The liberal trend appealed to the political expediency. By his religious policy Aurangzeb offered a huge bribe to orthodox clerical element and through their influence he hoped to rally all sections of the Muslims behind him. But the clerical element took advantage of the situation and started ammasing private fortunes. Even in the collection of *jaziya* Manucci informs us that the *amins* of *jaziya* keptback half or even three-fourth of the proceeds for themselves.[35]

---

53. Manucci, ii, 415; iii, 291.

The influence of the clerical section was very much resented by the Mughal Nobles and Grandees. As early as 1672 Mahabat Khan had protested by writing to the Emperor that "the Empire had become dependent on the Qazis." The same feeling is expressed in the remark of Mahabat Khan that instead of army being sent against Shivaji the task could be easily achieved by the *fatwa* of the *Qazi*. Such sentiments of the officers clearly indicete that they could not have been very enthusiastic in carrying Aurangzeb's wars of aggression and other administrative measures.

The religious plea taken by Aurangzeb also provided a similar slogan to such Hindu chiefs who were not serving under the Mughals or were trying to carve out their independent kingdoms on the crumbling structure of the empire. Shivaji could appeal to the Hindu sentiment and pose as their champion and protector. The coronation of Shivaji (6th June, 1674) characterised by observing the orthodox Hindu rites performed by Brahmins was almost a parallel declaration as that of Aurangzeb. The Brahmins were, like the ulama, richly rewarded of course within the means of Shivaji. Just as Shivaji's ideal of a *swaraj* "was based on orthodoxy, it contained within itself the seed of its own death", Aurangzeb's ideal of an Islamic state in India had the germs of consumption. Aurangzeb's religious policy created a division in the Indian society. At a lower level it brought about communal antagonism which became noticeable from such incidents as riots in Ujjain in 1671 or as a retaliation, "if the mosques did not escape the wrath of the Satnamis at Nornol (1672) or that of Rana Kunwar Bhim Singh, in the imperial territory of Gujarat (1681) the blame will have to go to Aurangzeb's policy of wrecking vengience upon the places of the worship of the enemies."[54]

The religious policy of Aurangzeb had its counterpart in Shivaji, and he did not fail to utilise even the incident of the

54. Rizvi, *Muslim Revivalist Movements in Northern India*, p. 387.

imposition of *jaziya*. He wrote to the Emperor a note of protest against the imposition of *jaziya*, knowing full well that a protest from him was meaningless for Aurangzeb. But by his protest he appealed to the Hindu sentiments and posed before them as a champion of their cause.

In the final analysis we find that both Aurangzeb and Shivaji, great personalities as they were, have left to the posterity a lasting lesson that a state founded and nurtured on sectarian and religious basis fails to acquire an enduring foundation.

INDEX